W9-BKL-552

STONY CREEK LIBRARY
1350 GREENFIELD PIKE
NOBLESVILLE, IN 46060

Amy Tan

Other titles in the *Authors Teens Love* series:

Ray Bradbury
Master of Science Fiction and Fantasy
ISBN-13: 978-0-7660-2240-9
ISBN-10:   0-7660-2240-4

Orson Scott Card
Architect of Alternate Worlds
ISBN-13: 978-0-7660-2354-3
ISBN-10:   0-7660-2354-0

Robert Cormier
Author of The Chocolate War
ISBN-13: 978-0-7660-2719-0
ISBN-10:   0-7660-2719-8

Roald Dahl
Author of Charlie and the Chocolate Factory
ISBN-13: 978-0-7660-2353-6
ISBN-10:   0-7660-2353-2

Paula Danziger
Voice of Teen Troubles
ISBN-13: 978-0-7660-2444-1
ISBN-10:   0-7660-2444-X

S. E. Hinton
Author of The Outsiders
ISBN-13: 978-0-7660-2720-6
ISBN-10:   0-7660-2720-1

C. S. Lewis
Chronicler of Narnia
ISBN-13: 978-0-7660-2446-5
ISBN-10:   0-7660-2446-6

Lois Lowry
The Giver of Stories and Memories
ISBN-13: 978-0-7660-2722-0
ISBN-10:   0-7660-2722-8

Joan Lowery Nixon
Masterful Mystery Writer
ISBN-13: 978-0-7660-2194-5
ISBN-10:   0-7660-2194-7

Gary Paulsen
Voice of Adventure and Survival
ISBN-13: 978-0-7660-2721-3
ISBN-10:   0-7660-2721-X

Richard Peck
A Spellbinding Storyteller
ISBN-13: 978-0-7660-2723-7
ISBN-10:   0-7660-2723-6

Philip Pullman
Master of Fantasy
ISBN-13: 978-0-7660-2447-2
ISBN-10:   0-7660-2447-4

Jerry Spinelli
Master Teller of Teen Tales
ISBN-13: 978-0-7660-2718-3
ISBN-10:   0-7660-2718-X

R. L. Stine
Creator of Creepy and Spooky Stories
ISBN-13: 978-0-7660-2445-8
ISBN-10:   0-7660-2445-8

J. R. R. Tolkien
Master of Imaginary Worlds
ISBN-13: 978-0-7660-2246-1
ISBN-10:   0-7660-2246-3

E. B. White
Spinner of Webs and Tales
ISBN-13: 978-0-7660-2350-5
ISBN-10:   0-7660-2350-8

AUTHORS TEENS LOVE

Amy Tan

Weaver of Asian-American Tales

Ann Angel

Enslow Publishers, Inc.
40 Industrial Road
Box 398
Berkeley Heights, NJ 07922
USA

http://www.enslow.com

Copyright © 2009 by Ann Angel

All rights reserved.

No part of this book may be reproduced by any means without the written permission of the publisher.

Library of Congress Cataloging-in-Publication Data

Angel, Ann, 1952-
   Amy Tan: weaver of Asian-American tales / Ann Angel.
       p. cm.—(Authors teens love)
   Includes bibliographical references and index.
   Summary: "A biography of Chinese-American author Amy Tan"—Provided by publisher.
   ISBN-13: 978-0-7660-2962-0
   ISBN-10: 0-7660-2962-X
   1. Tan, Amy—Juvenile literature. 2. Novelists, American—20th century—Biography—Juvenile literature. 3. Chinese Americans—Biography—Juvenile literature. I. Title.
   PS3570.A48Z54 2008
   813'.54—dc22
   [B]
                                                    2008012440

Printed in the United States of America

10 9 8 7 6 5 4 3 2 1

To Our Readers: We have done our best to make sure all Internet addresses in this book were active and appropriate when we went to press. However, the author and publisher have no control over and assume no liability for the material available on those Internet sites or on other Web sites they may link to. Any comments or suggestions can be sent by e-mail to comments@enslow.com or to the address on the back cover.

♻ Enslow Publishers, Inc., is committed to printing our books on recycled paper. The paper in every book contains 10% to 30% post-consumer waste (PCW). The cover board on the outside of each book contains 100% PCW. Our goal is to do our part to help young people and the environment too!

Illustration Credits: Copyright © by Amy Tan, reprinted by permission of the author and the Sandra Dijkstra Literary Agency, pp. 13, 15, 19, 22, 24, 31; AP/Wide World Photos, pp. 6, 44, 50; © Buena Vista Pictures/courtesy of the Everett Collection, p. 38; Getty Images for AFI, p. 88; Jupiterimages Corporation/Photos.com, pp. 72, 74; National Kidney Foundation of Northern California and Northern Nevada, p. 85.

Cover Illustration: Debra Rohlfs (background); WireImage/courtesy of Getty Images, Inc. (inset).

38888000189898

Contents

Chapter 1

The Sleepy Therapist

Although Amy Tan never thought about growing up to become a writer, imagination, luck, and a love of stories conspired to steer her to this fate. As a child, she thought she would become a successful doctor or concert pianist because these were her parents' hopes. In fact, Tan's evolution from a doctoral student in linguistics to a writer acclaimed for Chinese-American novels of mothers and daughters came about after a detour as a language development consultant and then as project director for programs serving disabled students. She actually credits failed therapy sessions for her self-described workaholism in writing fiction. According to Tan, when her therapist fell asleep for the third time, she decided she could use the two hundred dollars a session in better ways and signed up with the Squaw Valley Community of Writers.[1]

Tan turned in a short story for critique and was encouraged to keep writing by her earliest mentor and editor, Molly Giles. Tan described her relationship and first meeting with Giles. "Molly's always been a great editor and friend. She's been my editor since my first attempts at writing. She read one of my first stories and said, 'Well, this is

---

An Award-Winning Writing Mentor

Tan's first mentor, Molly Giles, has notable ranking among writers herself. Nominated for a Pulitzer Prize for her first short-story collection, *Rough Translations*, she is also the recipient of the Flannery O'Connor Award for Short Fiction, the California Book Award for Short Fiction, and the Small Press Best Fiction/Short Story Award. Giles, one of the most popular creative writing teachers at San Francisco State University, routinely taught oversubscribed classes while also mentoring such writers as Tan, Gus Lee, and Melba Beals. Giles loves teaching and although she would never want to give it up completely, she has admitted, "It's always a struggle to teach and to write."[2]

In addition to writing two collections of short stories, Giles is credited with writing *Iron Shoes*, a novel said to be written with "such intelligence and wit, that the book flares and sparkles with unexpected insight."[3]

---

a story and this is another story and there's a third. Pick one and take it slowly.'"[4]

The Squaw Valley Writers Workshop, where Tan met Giles, was only the first step in a path to writing her novels. "Going to the workshop didn't confirm that I had any special talent," Tan once told an interviewer, "but it confirmed that I could learn to do this as a craft, and that learning that in itself was completely fulfilling."[5]

The short story Tan submitted in 1986 to Giles's workshop would be developed over time into *The Joy Luck Club*, a novel that stayed on the *New York Times* best-seller list for nine months and was honored as a National Book Award finalist.[6] But before that, Tan's first short story, "End Game," was published in a now-defunct magazine *PM Five*. The story was later reprinted in *Seventeen* where one of the country's most respected agents, Sandra Dijkstra, saw it. She encouraged Tan to keep writing. Tan wrote three more stories and gave them to Dijkstra, who submitted them along with a proposal for a collection to Putnam editor Faith Sales. Sales contracted Tan for a book of short stories that became *The Joy Luck Club*, which was published in 1989.[7]

While often surmising that her success as an author could be fate or luck, Tan is quick to credit the many people who helped with her career. Editor Faith Sales remained a constant in Tan's life until her death in 1999.[8]

Tan believes that fortune, or luck, and fate have led her to success in her writing. But fate

Is She Speaking for the Chinese-American Culture?

Living in San Francisco and writing about her relationship with her mother, Tan never even considered that she was writing about the Chinese-American culture. She simply tells the stories she knows—stories about mothers and daughters, stories about her own relationship with her mother.

alone seems to have led her from that PhD program in linguistics to writing. Initially, it was not a positive fate, but the violent death of a friend that initiated this journey.

On a February night in 1976, Tan's close friend and former housemate, a Wisconsinite named Pete, was murdered during a robbery. Tan recognized that Pete's life had been filled with meaning because he had chosen to work with disadvantaged youth. "A valuable life had been lost," Tan recalled, "and to make up for it, I had to find value in mine."[9]

After his death, Tan believed that Pete guided her life to change through her dreams. It was his guidance, she has said, that led her to a job in a California county program as a language development specialist working with children and their families.

While Tan made the happy change and began to find value in her own life, Pete's murderers were caught and a trial was held, convicting one person of first-degree murder. Meanwhile, Tan's life seemed to settle into a routine of days filled with observing children, assessing their communication abilities, and creating plans to meet their needs. Pete arrived in one more dream.

In this dream, he told Tan to connect to a friend of his named Rose, telling her that Rose would become very important to her. "She's a writer," he said, "and she'll be helpful to you when you become a writer."[10] She and Rose did connect. Tan had the good fortune of Rose's guidance, offering Tan reading suggestions for her inspiration. As fate would have it, Tan immersed herself in her work with children for seven more years—but as a technical writer of special programs. While she was satisfied that she was making a difference, Tan discovered she was also becoming into a workaholic. She became increasingly more concerned about the amount of time and energy she put into this field. Even as Tan's discontent led her into therapy, Rose became the first person to encourage Tan to write fiction. Rose even offered suggestions for submitting her earliest attempts. Nevertheless, Tan's technical writing filled more and more of her free time in her efforts to become the success her parents had always envisioned. Finally, Tan sought psychotherapy for her workaholism.[11]

Whether it is fate or fortune that allowed Tan to follow this winding path to telling her stories, it is fortunate indeed for those who love Tan's work that her therapist fell asleep.

Chapter 2

From China to the United States

Amy Tan's history spans China and the United States. As Tan herself admitted, the story of her background is shrouded in her mother's secrets. Tan learned of these stories through hints and shaded comments while growing up with her widowed mother. Tan's history only took on clarity when she began to share her fiction with her mother. When Tan read the stories of women who were forced into marriages, became young widows, or were beaten until they escaped, Tan's mother asked how she knew these specific details about her grandmother and great-aunts and their difficult, grief-filled lives.

The truth is that, while she was growing up, Tan's grandmother was only the face of a solemn child named Jingmei in a photograph taken in

Amy Tan's grandmother Gu Jingmei (left) with an unidentified relative in Shanghai, China, circa 1905.

China. That child, dressed in traditional Chinese clothes, did not seem to have much connection to Tan, an American-Chinese girl who wanted to leave the old traditions behind. But in writing, as Tan looked back at her grandmother's life, she realized that her Chinese grandmother's life formed the basis of her relationship with her mother. Her grandmother's story became the impetus for many of Tan's stories. They were stories of women caught between two cultures. It was the weave of those cultures that controlled Tan's mother's choices, beliefs, and ideals, and those same aspects of Tan's own life.

Tan has learned that her grandmother Jingmei married a poor scholar who died suddenly around 1918. He probably died of the flu as that was the year of the big flu pandemic. Tan's mother, the second child and first daughter named Du Ching or Daisy,[1] was born to this scholar and Jingmei in Hangzhou in about 1916.

A few years after Tan's grandfather died, a rich man "who liked to collect pretty women" saw Jingmei while she was on an outing. According to Tan, this rich man manipulated it so that one of his many wives invited Jingmei to be a guest at their home. He raped her, which made her an outcast within her culture, a culture that prized pure women. She left her son, her firstborn, to be raised by his paternal relatives, but she took her daughter, Daisy, to live in the rich man's house where she resided as a concubine. Shortly after Jingmei gave birth to the rich man's only son, she killed

Amy Tan's mother, Daisy (center), around age eight, in Hangzhou, China, circa 1924.

herself by eating opium that had been cooked into New Year's rice cakes. On her deathbed, she told Daisy who wept at her side, "Don't follow my footsteps." Tan's mother was sent to be raised by her mother's sisters. She kept this story a secret most of her life.[2]

"We know the past can be changed," Tan says of the lessons she learned through the story of her grandmother's life. "We can choose what we should believe. We can choose what we should remember. That is what frees us, this choice, frees us to hope that we can redeem these same memories for the little girl who became my mother."[3]

Tan's mother never lost her shame that her own mother had been a concubine. She never told even her closest friends, and she would frequently caution Tan not to tell others, reminding Tan that Jingmei was really a woman of class who had no other choices in her life.[4]

Amy's own mother had a secret Chinese past. Until Amy, who was born on February 19, 1952 in the United States, was about ten, she had no idea that her mother had been married once before in China.[5] And, like her mother, Daisy left behind her children. Amy's mother's closest friends had no knowledge of this marriage to a pilot, Wang Zo, who was honored as a Kuomintang (Nationalist Party) hero but who Daisy claimed was evil. "He was no hero," Daisy once told Amy. "He was dismissed from the air force for bad morals."[6]

But at nineteen, Daisy was a beautiful and innocent young woman, spoiled from early on because of her beauty. Just as a bad man had been attracted to her own mother for her beauty, it was Daisy's beauty that brought her the ill fortune of marrying a man who was so bad he was seen with another woman the day before he married her. After Daisy and Wang Zo were married, he would bring women to his house and openly humiliate Daisy.

Despite the difficulties of her marriage and even with three young children in tow, Daisy was a beautiful woman. In 1941, she met Amy's father, John Tan, while taking a day trip on a boat. They were immediately attracted to each other. Despite the attraction, Daisy dutifully returned to her husband. She and John were not to see each other or be together for four more years until they ran into each other walking down the street in Tientsin. Then they admitted their earlier attraction. Daisy later reminisced, "It was fate."[7]

But at the time, when Daisy attempted to run away with John, Wang Zo had Daisy jailed and tried for adultery.[8]

John, who would later father Amy, was born in 1913, the oldest of twelve children. His mother was a traditional Chinese healer, but his father, Hugh Tan, became a Presbyterian minister after being converted by missionaries who taught him in the English-speaking schools in Canton.

A devout Baptist and gifted scholar, John Tan was offered scholarships to colleges in the United States. While Daisy was still in jail, and despite his love for Daisy, John immigrated to California and took a scholarship at MIT. According to Amy, he attended the First Chinese Baptist Church and lived at the YMCA. But at night, when he should have been studying, John Tan would find himself writing in a diary about the sins of his past. The woman he loved was in jail and he was honest enough with himself to acknowledge that he had committed adultery.

It was through this self-study that John decided to leave MIT and instead devote himself to saving others. He enrolled in the Berkeley Baptist Divinity School and Amy says his faith, from that day forward, was absolute. While studying at the divinity school, John often spent time innocently with the single women of his parish who were eager to court this divinity student. According to photos, they often picnicked in area parks or went to dances. According to Amy, her father was "a good catch; a superb dancer, a witty conversationalist, a man given to romantic gestures and eternal pledges."[9]

Then in 1949, in the midst of China's fall to communism, he was able to bring Daisy to the United States after she was released from jail where she had served two years for adultery. In his mind, "It was God's will and some other woman's bad luck."[10] A son, Peter, was born in 1950.[11] Amy was born two years later, on February 19, 1952, the year of the dragon, after her parents had moved to the San Francisco Bay area in Oakland, California. Amy grew up surrounded by the tension between her father's Christian

Amy Tan's parents, John and Daisy, in Tientsin, China, 1945.

beliefs and her mother's strong belief in Chinese superstitions.[12]

"My father prayed. My mother looked at *everything*," Amy says. Amy rejected all beliefs back then. She says this is probably what made her a writer.[13]

Within the Tan family, Amy was the middle of three children, with Peter the eldest, and a younger brother, John, whom the family referred to as Didi, which is Chinese for "little brother."[14]

Amy does not recall ever thinking as a child that she wanted to become a writer, although she wrote in class like everyone else did. The thought did not even enter her mind when she was eight and won an essay contest sponsored by the Citizens for Santa Rosa Library for her essay "What the Library Means to Me."[15]

When she was about ten, Amy's mother revealed that she had been married once before. Amy found out that she was actually one of eight children. She learned that during Daisy's first marriage to Wang Zo, Daisy had given birth to five additional children. Amy's oldest half sisters include Yuhang, who is sixteen years older than Amy, Jindo, and Li Jung. One half sister died at birth and a half brother also died in China when he was a child.[16]

Perhaps because Daisy had lost so much, she placed all of her hopes on her children, pushing them toward success and prestige. Despite Amy's wish to be an artist and her ability to love to lose herself in fiction, Amy was told she would grow up

Books Open Windows to the World

When she was eight, Amy won first prize in her age group with an essay she wrote extolling the local library. She received a transistor radio, and the essay was published in her local paper. The essay, published in the *Santa Rosa Press Democrat*, said: "I love to read. My father takes me to the library every two weeks, and I check out five or six books each time. These books seem to open many windows in my little room." According to Amy, she was so earnest about the library and this essay contest that she donated her entire life savings of eighteen cents to the library fund.[18]

"For me, reading was a refuge. I could escape from everything that was miserable in my life and I could be anyone I wanted to be in a story, through a character," says Amy. "It was almost sinful how much I liked it."[19]

to be a doctor and, in her spare time, a concert pianist. She buried her creative desires. Still, she had doubts about her future plans. "I wasn't that good a pianist and I didn't know if I really wanted to help people who were sick and had diseases. I didn't know if that was really in me, let alone if I could pass a science course," she says.[17]

There were teachers who inspired Amy to consider the choices she might make with her life. One in particular was her third-grade teacher, Ms.

Amy Tan at eight years old (foreground) being congratulated for her essay "What the Library Means to Me" in Santa Rosa, California, 1960.

Grudoff. There had been talk that year of allowing Amy to skip a grade because she had already learned the multiplication tables and had read the required books. Amy was never sure who decided that might be bad for her psychologically, but she remained in third grade. When class lessons became repetitive, Ms. Grudoff encouraged Amy to go the back of the room to draw pictures. "I didn't become an artist," recalls Amy, "but some-body let me do something I loved. What a luxury, to do something you love to do."[20]

Amy's parents maintained high expectations for all their children. They expected straight A's even in kindergarten so that Amy grew up feeling tremendous pressure to achieve and, as an adult, does not recall many openly affectionate moments. Her mother's difficult childhood and having seen her own mother commit suicide made Daisy less nurturing than most mothers. Amy recalls that at the funeral of a childhood playmate, while Amy stood at the casket staring at her friend's body in repose, her mother leaned over and said, "This is what happens when you don't listen to your mother."[21]

Amy is quick to point out that her mother had been raised in an atmosphere of fear and so she used it to try to control her own children. In this story of the deceased playmate, Amy believes her mother was warning Amy to wash fruit before eating it, something this dead playmate had possibly failed to do. With current studies proving

Amy Tan at twelve years old posing with her cat Fufu.

that pesticides can cause cancer and leukemia, Amy believes her mother might have been right.[22]

The family's early years were fraught with disagreement over practicing the piano, which Amy disliked, over homework, and more. Amy once wrote her mother a letter, telling her: "I hate you." She called her a witch. Then Amy packed up a treasure box with a photo of her dad, but not her mom, and ran away. Her mother found her and

---

Ghosts of Her Mother's Past

Often, when Amy misbehaved, her mother threatened suicide or threatened to return to China to her other children. Amy's adolescence was tense and anxiety ridden. Amy now believes her mother was only acting out of the experiences of her own life. Daisy had only been nine when she witnessed her mother's suicide.

After Amy's brother and then her father both died when she was sixteen, Daisy often insisted that Amy operate a Ouija board to communicate with the spirits of departed family members, including Daisy's mother, grandmother, and husband, always seeking reassurance that Daisy's fate was turning for the better and that she was still loved from the other side. She worried about the forces that seemed to be aligned against the family, and she believed a curse on the family had led to the deaths of her husband and son.[23]

---

brought her back. Recalling a moment when Daisy demonstrated her maternal love for her daughter, Amy said, "She made tuna fish for me." This was Amy's favorite sandwich.[24]

In 1967, when Amy was sixteen, her older brother Peter died of a brain tumor. Sadly and ironically, her father also died of a brain tumor the next year, 1968.[25]

While her father and brother were dying, Amy kept a journal. "I was losing hope and no one would admit that they were also losing hope," she says. "I listed the top 100 hits. It was very trivial. I needed to focus on something that had nothing to do with the rest of the world. If someone were to read that now, they would think, 'Oh, what a shallow girl.'"[26]

After her father's death, possibly to escape a similar fate, Daisy Tan moved her surviving son, John, and daughter as far away as possible, to Montreux, Switzerland.[27] Amy recalled that the move to Switzerland was "so preposterously different that she [her mother] knew she had to give up grieving simply to survive." But Amy also recalled that her mother remained terribly sad.[28]

This was also a difficult time for the sixteen-year-old, who sought solace in books, such as Charlotte Brontë's *Jane Eyre*, Louise Erdrich's *Love Medicine*, and Vladimir Nabokov's *Lolita*. Nabokov fascinated Amy with his wit and parody.[29] She also found comfort with a boyfriend, a German army deserter named Franz.[30] Amy struggled to get along with her mother at this time but their arguments became increasingly more destructive.[31] One time, Amy's mother, furious because she did not believe Franz was a good person, ordered Amy to stop seeing him and even slapped her. "I rather kill myself before I see you destroy your life!" her mother warned. This was such an old threat, as Amy had heard her mother threaten suicide countless times before, so she refused to stop seeing Franz. The argument escalated until Amy's mother threatened to kill Amy.[32]

Under her mother's watchful eye and protectiveness, Tan believes now that she learned to fear much about the world. She says that even as a little girl, "I remember thinking there were things wrong with the world." But as a teen, "I didn't want it that way. I measured danger everywhere."[33]

Tan recalled another especially heated argument when she screamed at her mother, "I hate you. I wish you were dead."[34]

While her mother usually responded that maybe she would follow Amy's father and brother in death, sometimes, she carried her threats a bit further and made futile attempts to end her own life. Tan recalls her mother running into the street, putting a knife to her throat, claiming she had storms in her chest. "For days after our arguments," Tan wrote in an essay about her mother, "she would not speak to me. She tormented me, acted as if she had no feelings for me whatsoever."[35]

Tan realizes when she looks back that, with each dour warning, her mother, who only meant to protect her, actually pushed her and pushed her toward the very things her mother did not want. In response to her mother's fears, Tan says, "I did everything."[36]

It was the very fact that Franz was forbidden to her that made Amy want him more.[37] Eventually Amy realized that life with Franz was not quite the romantic ideal she craved. But when she attempted to break up with Franz, he threatened to throw himself beneath a train. Fearing the worst, Amy agreed to run away with Franz and get married. Amy must have realized that her pending college applications were more important because she called her mother and warned that she and Franz were about to elope. Amy's mother and the police arrived before the couple boarded the train. A short time later, a small cache of illegal drugs was found stashed in a Volkswagon van that Franz and his friends owned; he was found guilty of drug possession and deported.

Still, Franz held intrigue and, when a letter arrived for Amy, the fighting between her mother and herself escalated once again. Finally, Amy's mother offered to take her to the border so she could be with Franz. Tan now says, "The intrigue of this guy being forbidden to me was gone. I saw him as dirty. Frayed."[38]

The court magistrate, who had found Franz guilty, allowed Amy to return home but only after promising to obey her mother and never again give her a single defiant word. Amy went back to the international school where she prepared her college applications and immersed herself in her studies. She graduated in her junior year in 1969. Because of all the moves the family made, it was the eleventh school Amy had attended.[39]

"My life is, I believe, excellent fodder for fiction," Tan once wrote. "Memory feeds imagination, and my imagination is glutted with a Thanksgiving of nightmares."[40]

How Do Teenagers See the World?

Tan understands that parents worry and want to protect their children. In contrast, she believes teenagers want the world to be a nicer place than their parents warn them against. "It's not about seeing the world as bad, but there are things out there," she said. "Teenagers don't want to have calluses yet." How can parents give their teenagers a way to see the world so that they can keep their hearts? she asked. She responded with another question: "How can we have them see the world in a fresh way and make their own choices?"[41]

Chapter 3

Finding Stories in The Joy Luck Club

After graduating from high school, Tan returned to the United States to attend Linfield College in McMinnville, Oregon, as an American Baptist Scholar, which she often points out with irony, that despite her relationship with Franz, was a scholarship for her "high morals."[1]

While she was a student at Linfield, Tan met her husband, Lou DeMattei, who was studying to become a tax attorney,[2] on a blind date.[3] The two moved to San Jose where Tan enrolled in San Jose City College. She then transferred to San Jose State University where she became an English honors student and a President's Scholar, worked two part-time jobs, and received a BA with a double major in linguistics and English in 1972. After attending the Summer Linguistics Institute at the

Amy Tan and Lou DeMattei in 1974, the year they were married.

University of California, Santa Cruz, on a scholarship, Tan earned an MA in linguistics from San Jose State University. She began doctoral studies in linguistics at The University of California, Berkeley, with a Graduate Minority Fellowship under the affirmative-action program. In all, Tan attended five colleges.[4]

While still a student, Tan married DeMattei in 1974 and the two shared an apartment with a roommate, Pete, for a time. But before long, Pete moved into a place of his own to focus on improving the lives of less advantaged children. His murder during a robbery turned Tan's life upside down. After reflecting on the meaning of her own life and how she could do something meaningful, Tan left the graduate program without obtaining her degree and dedicated herself to creating individualized educational programs for school children with speech and language deficits.

She worked relentlessly for the next five years as a language development consultant and project director for programs serving disabled children from birth through age five. At first, she wrote plans to mainstream students, then she wrote grant proposals to gain funding for special programs for these students. She was good at this sort of writing, so she became a freelance business writer specializing in corporate communications for such companies as AT&T and Pacific Bell. Tan took on more and more freelance business until it began to overwhelm her. It was at this point in her life that she realized she was spending all of her time working but with little satisfaction.[5]

This is when she turned to therapy to resolve her self-described workaholic tendencies. She complained to her Jungian therapist that she was writing corporate communications ninety hours per week but still felt the need to take on more and more work, "to prove something about who I am."[6]

In those sessions, Tan recalled how she reclined on a couch while the psychiatrist sat behind her, listening and never uttering a word. Tan often retells the story, using a tone that belies her amusement, of how this experience led to writing fiction. "About three months into it, I turned around and saw he was asleep. It took about two more times before I realized I should just quit."[7]

Tan turned to reading fiction as a way to balance her life. After all, she had been an English major and had loved to study words. She had always enjoyed reading, so she immersed herself in books.[8]

Reading finally led Tan to what she termed "self-help therapy" in the form of fiction writing when she happened upon the Squaw Valley Writers conference and signed up for a workshop. "It was the process that I knew I wanted to do for the rest of my life." Tan realized that she might discover that she did not have any special talent to be published, but publication was beside the point. "I loved talking about fiction with other writers, and the more we talked about things the more excited I got. As we critiqued each other's work, I felt I was able to see my own work at another level."[9]

Tan immediately respected the insights of her workshop leader, Molly Giles. "She would make a remark that would resonate with me, and I'd work on it," Tan said.[10]

Under Giles's guidance and then the guidance of her California writers' group, Tan wrote short stories that reflected her own understanding of Chinese-American mothers and daughters.[11]

It was while she was working on the stories that Tan and her mother made their first trip to China where Tan met the three half sisters her mother had been forced to abandon years before. "I went from a very small family to a very large family," Tan said. Always able to see the humor in the turns her life takes, she added, "It makes it hard to get dinner reservations, I'll tell you that."[12]

Although Tan revised each story at least twenty times, she felt as though the stories that comprise *The Joy Luck Club* were a gift to her from an invisible storyteller. "When I wrote these stories, it was as much a discovery to me as to any reader reading them for the first time. Things would surprise me."[13]

With only one story written, Tan attracted an agent, Sandy Dijkstra, who encouraged her to continue writing about the characters that became the four sets of mothers and daughter in *The Joy Luck Club*.[14]

An Editor and Friend

It did not take long for Sandra Dijkstra to sell Tan's short stories as the beginning of a novel to an editor who saw the impact they might have on readers. Tan's editor for *The Joy Luck Club* and most of her future novels was Faith Sales, famous for being involved in the lives of her writers. Sales understood that a writer's work reflected who she was as a person. She and Tan became close friends. "She was like a second mother," Tan once said, "and then she died. . . ."[15]

A series of collages about the lives and relationships between four American-born Chinese women and their immigrant mothers, the novel includes details from Tan's life and details of stories she had heard. Tan set out to write the stories for her mother to help the two understand and, possibly resolve, the cultural and generational misunderstandings and disagreements in their lives together. "I wanted her to know what I thought about China and what I thought about growing up in this country. And I wanted those words to almost fall off the page so that she could just see the story."[16]

The novel captures Tan's own experience growing up in America, a world that is completely different from the one her mother knew growing up in China. Her life and stories are an experience that creates discomfort with old customs and traditions for the young while the mothers place all of their hopes in their daughters.

In short vignettes, alternating between the lives of four Chinese mothers and their American-born daughters, one of the daughters named June "begins to understand the real dimensions of the 'unspeakable tragedies they had left behind in China.'" After the death of her mother, June "begins to see her mother's generation in a different light." Through the discovery of her mother's harsh suffering and her escape to the United States, June learns why her mother and the other three mothers have placed so much hope and pride in their American-born daughters' success. One reviewer said, "The book is a meditation on the divided nature of the emigrant life."[17]

The novel's theme of reaching understandings between time and cultures is captured in the opening scene with the image of a swan's white feather, a metaphor for the mothers' stories. "For a long time now the woman had wanted to give her daughter the single swan feather and tell her, 'This feather may look worthless, but it comes from afar and carries with it all my good intentions.' And she waited, year after year, for the day she could tell her daughter this with perfect American English."[18]

Although this scene opens the novel, it was the very last scene that Tan wrote.[19]

The Joy Luck Club debuted on March 22, 1989, and hit the *New York Times* best-seller list about four weeks later. The novel's success was a shock to Tan who could never have expected this sort of attention. "I kept thinking that it was a fluke and it would stop. I was telling my husband that the average shelf life of a book was six weeks, and it would be over . . . and it just kept going and going . . . it was nerve-wracking! It wasn't until October that I recognized that it was not going away, and that I'd probably be able to write fiction for the rest of my life if I wanted to."[20]

Even more amazing, before the novel arrived on bookstore shelves, it was optioned as a movie in 1988.[21] Tan described her understanding of how this turn of events evolved. "They [movie producers] get these manuscripts and somebody makes copies and they send them out to people in Hollywood. Then you start hearing from people even before a book comes out. So I met with somebody from Oliver Stone's office long before the book ever came out and they were just stories. . . . She [the producer] got it when no one was supposed to see it, only my editor and my agent."[22]

The Joy Luck Club remained on the best-seller list for nine months and went on to become a 1989 National Book Award finalist.[23]

Originally, Tan had no intention of working on the film, but she ended up co-writing the screenplay after Ron Bass encouraged her. "Ron said, 'I really think you'd learn something creatively that will really help you in the other things that you'd do.'"[24]

The eight stars of the 1993 movie adaptation of *The Joy Luck Club*: (left to right) Kieu Chinh, Ming-Na Wen, Tamlyn Tomita, Tsai Chin, France Nuyen, Lauren Tom, Lisa Lu, and Rosalind Chao.

Filming *The Joy Luck Club*

Some of the women whose stories Tan had fictionalized tried out for roles in the film. Most were cast in small roles, which seemed to satisfy each of them. Tan's relatives also made cameo appearances. Her four-year-old niece, Melissa, received a speaking role as the daughter of Rose. Tan's Auntie Jayne and Uncle Tuck were cast as dinner guests in another scene. Amy's mother served as an extra in a party scene that begins and ends the film. Tan herself was cast in two parts of the film, but only one scene made it to the final production. In that party scene, Tan plays the role of her cowriter's wife. They can be spotted walking into the party while Bass is talking on a cell phone and Tan is apologizing for being late.[25]

Although the film was sold before the book came out, Tan and Bass did not begin writing the screenplay until 1991. In October 1992, actual filming began. Finally, in February 1993, Tan flew to China at her own expense to participate in filming that took place there.[26]

It was not until April of 1993 that Tan saw the first cut of the film. She admitted that she laughed and cried. In her essay about the filming, Tan said, "I've now seen the movie about twenty-five times, and I am not ashamed to say I've been moved to tears each time."[27]

It turned out that Bass was right and Tan thoroughly enjoyed leaning about making filmmaking. Little did she know this would only be the first time she allowed a creative suggestion to lead her into new media. But right now, there was another novel to write, and, with all her success, a new worry began to nag at Tan. How would she top this with a second novel?[28]

Despite her immediate success, Tan continued to meet weekly with her writers' group after the novel's publication, and she began work on a second novel. The writers continued to serve as her first group of readers. "I learned to listen," she says of her time with them. "I learned to see fiction."[29]

Little did Tan realize, even though the novel remained on the best-seller list and won awards, that *The Joy Luck Club* would become required reading in high school and college classrooms. It remains a popular and important book for many women and for many reasons.

Twenty years after its publication, Senator Hillary Clinton told Oprah Winfrey that *The Joy Luck Club* was one of the most important books she had ever read. She said, "This novel opened my eyes, not only to the distinct and special traditions of the Chinese-American culture but also to the ways in which immigrant women of different generations adopted and adjusted to life in this country."[30]

Chapter 4

The Kitchen God's Wife

Despite her success, Tan was determined to keep everything in her life the same. Soon, though, Tan noticed that people began to stop before her first-floor home and point. She said the mailman would even tell neighbors about her mail. She felt exposed and soon she and her husband, Lou DeMattei, a tax attorney, moved a few blocks away to a third-floor condominium. Demand grew for interviews, and Tan discovered her public personality to be much different from her private behavior. Others noticed this, too. One reporter commented, "She is trying very hard to be outgoing and cheerful, but her nervousness shows."[1]

Nervousness aside, Tan proved charismatic in crowds. She preferred a simple "art-student hip" style and "artful silver jewelry." Her quiet demeanor and style drew everyone's attention whenever she walked into a room. Her friend Asa MeMatteo once commented, "I remember once being at a party and Amy came in with a model friend of hers, a corn-fed, blue-eyed blonde. I believe Amy was wearing a black leotard and a pair of old bib overalls—something like that. Amy was the one everybody wanted to talk to."[2]

While fame may have made her quieter, Tan always handles herself with grace. But Tan herself noticed that she was now more comfortable and much sillier in private settings.[3]

Tan seemed to feel the pressure of success in the way she worked, too. She wrote everyday, usually for six to eight hours. But there were days when Tan worked so diligently, she closed the curtains in her office and had no clue if the sun had set. On those days, she worked around the clock.[4]

There was some frustration in her efforts to create her next novel. Tan wrote hundreds of pages for seven novels before coming up with the story for *The Kitchen God's Wife*.[5]

But Tan learned from these challenges. She said, "I don't look at those pages as failed stories. I see them as my own personal version of cautionary tales—what can happen if I *do* watch out, what can go wrong if I write as the author everyone thought I had become and not as the writer I truly was."[6]

It took her mother's voice for Tan to realize what her story was to become. "My mother kept complaining about how she had to tell everybody that she was not the model for the mother in *The Joy Luck Club*," Tan said, "She told me that next time I should write her true story."[7]

It was then that Tan asked her mother to tell the story of her life. Her mother poured out the way her own mother's suicide created a legacy of unhappiness, and she told of the hardships facing women and families in China during World War II. Tan heard the details of Daisy's marriage to a man who she referred to as "that bad man" and his abusive behavior. It finally drove Daisy to flee China, leaving behind her three daughters, whom Tan had met when she was in her thirties, shortly before publication of *The Joy Luck Club*.

While Tan recorded her mother's stories, she became aware that she had never listened to the stories the way her mother had wanted her to. "She wanted someone to go back and relive her life with her. It was a way for her to exorcize her demons, and for me to finally listen and empathize and learn what memory means, and what you can change about the past."[8]

When a *New York Times'* reporter heard this story, she concluded that the difficult life between mother and daughter contributed to Tan and Lou DeMattei's decision not to have children. During that interview, Tan commented, "I remember being such an unhappy child and I can't guarantee that I won't do the same things my mother did."[9]

The tragic, sad, heartwarming, sometimes humorous stories Tan heard as a child coupled with her own mother and daughter experiences

Choosing Not to Have Children

Tan has said in at least one interview that at first the choice not to have children was simply a decision to think about it later. She never felt she needed to replicate herself through children and she did not think it would make her marriage more complete. She does not regret not having children, although she sometimes thinks she has missed out on a kind of love she could not have with anyone else. In the end, though, Tan concluded, "I was also able to have this other kind of life that I experience through writing."[10]

Amy Tan and husband Lou DeMattei may not have children, but they have cared for several Yorkshire terriers over the years. Tan poses in her New York apartment with Bubba on her right in 2005.

became the focus of her second novel. *The Kitchen God's Wife*, published by Putnam Books in 1991, is the story of an immigrant Chinese woman who tells her daughter the story of the oppression of women in China before the revolution.[11]

The novel, a story of secrets revealed, opens with Winnie Louie's suspicions that her daughter Pearl is keeping secrets from her just as Winnie has kept secrets from her Chinese-American daughter. When Winnie reveals the secrets of abandonment by her own mother and a previous marriage in China, Pearl realizes that her mother's intrusiveness and humorlessness come out of the painful events of her early experiences.[12]

Writing *The Kitchen God's Wife* taught Tan about the importance of analyzing her own work and about the craft of writing. She said in an interview about the novel, "I see all the faults. I know what's been put in and what's been taken out. I know where the mistakes are, and I'm always afraid someone's going to catch them and say, 'You put the wrong emphasis on this,' or 'You used the wrong angle on that.'"[13]

While she had felt pressure to create a second great novel, she believes most of the pressure was self-induced. She was driven by a need to "create something that was different, yet honest, personally meaningful, and which contained the aesthetic merits I valued in good fiction." To further heighten her anxiety about the book's potential success, Tan often remembered old, and usually bad, book reviews. She worried because she did not want to

To Be a Woman in Feudal China

Tan visited China a number of times to gather research on women in that country. She learned that the philosophy of Confucius, which was practiced in China for more than one thousand years, preached that women were inferior to men. Women in China were denied education and expected to obey the men who dominated their lives. A girl growing up in China was considered the private property of men and believed her role was to please her husband and bear children. Her feet were bound, and she obeyed her father until she was married in an arranged marriage. Divorce was not allowed and remarriage if the woman became widowed was unheard of. A woman obeyed her husband, and widows were expected to obey their male children. This practice existed until well into the twentieth century when the People's Republic of China was established under the Communist Party, which recognized the liberation of women.[14]

Still, despite liberation, women in China continued to face harsh obstacles. In 1998, their unemployment rate was about 60 percent. As many as 70 percent of the 140 million illiterate Chinese citizens were female because peasant families, continued to practice feudal traditions and refused to send their daughters to school.[15]

disappoint her publisher with a less successful book. Finally, Tan had to quiet her fears and just write a book. The result was a successful second novel that appealed to women and their daughters. While Tan admits the anxiety gets worse with each book she writes, she was acclaimed for this novel and described as a writer who captures the complexities of mother-daughter relationships.[16]

Ghosts in Her Life

After the publication of *The Kitchen God's Wife*, Tan set to work on her third novel. While she worked, she recognized that, although tragic experiences had changed her life, it was luck, coincidence, and perhaps even spirits or ghosts that made her wonder about life and afterlife.

She once told a reporter that she believed ghosts would occasionally visit her 1916 town house. Tan playfully reported the spirits clomped down steps, made noises, slammed doors, and harassed decorators she had hired. "Whenever a decorator comes here to do something connected to the wiring," Amy said, "they always run into trouble."[17]

Tan looks back and sees that her writing career could not have been better at this time. Her first book had been nominated for awards and remained a best seller. Now her second novel climbed best-seller lists. At the same time, the film adaptation of *The Joy Luck Club* was scheduled to debut and initial reviews were promising. Tan should have been happy. Instead, she felt "crushing depression." On the night of the film's premiere, she recalls, "I was standing on the balcony of my hotel room thinking, life is meaningless, this is all stupid, jump now before you change your mind. I realized I needed help."[18]

Tan learned she was suffering from depression as a result of past tragedies, including the deaths of her father and brother and the murder of her friend Pete. Antidepressants helped her cope with the posttraumatic stress of these events. Tan told a reporter that she recognized these profound experiences changed her life. She said, "I just keep reminding myself how lucky I am each day."[19]

Chapter 5

A Band of Bookmakers

Between book tours and trying to find time to work on two children's books she had agreed to write, Tan found it increasingly difficult to schedule private time into her busy life. Relieved to return home in November 1991, Tan was surprised to receive a fax from her media escort, Kathi Kamen Goldmark, inviting her to join the Rock Bottom Remainders. The planned rock band would include writers Stephen King, Dave Berry, and Barbara Kingsolver.[1]

The band's name was planned to reflect the literary leanings of its members. The term remainder is a publishing term referring to books that have not sold well at regular prices or best sellers that are no longer in demand. Publishers sell

Amy Tan in a blonde wig and horror author Stephen King on guitar rock out with the Rock Bottom Remainders in King's hometown of Bangor, Maine, to raise funds for a local charity.

them at discount prices and the books are called remainders.

Tan said of that November 6 fax, "I pondered that fax. Did I look like the kind of writer who had time for a lot of fun? As to singing in public, could there be anything more similar to a public execution?"[2]

She agreed to join and has remained a constant presence in the group.[3]

Billing themselves as a literary garage band, the group performs to raise funds for America Scores, an after school literacy program for inner city kids.[4]

America Scores uses the lessons of teamwork from soccer to encourage students in their creative writing. The students have even become involved in the band's media events. When a press conference is held, many of the children attend and read poetry.

In 2007, the band created the "Still Younger Than Keith Tour" and scheduled a June appearance at Book Expo in New York City. Funds raised here were planned to benefit 826 NYC, Get Caught Reading, and The American Booksellers Foundation for Free Expression.[5]

Although the Rock Bottom Remainders do not have an album, they are periodically recognized as one of the most ragtag of rock bands, the group boasts over 150 million books sold, and their books have been translated into more than twenty-five languages.[6]

Barbara Kingsolver took a leave for a time but

These Boots Are Made for Walking

Tan became legend in the Rock Bottom Remainders for sporting a red wig and wearing tall black leather boots while belting out Nancy Sinatra's signature song, "These Boots Are Made for Walking."[7]

additional writers have joined the group. Most recently, Greg Iles, whose novel *24 Hours* was made into a movie, joined the band as bass player.[8]

Additional band members have included sports writer Mitch Albom and *The Simpsons* television show creator Matt Groening. The members originally intended to organize to raise money as a one-time effort. But they enjoyed themselves so much and became so popular that they continue to tour together and have raised more than $1 million for children's charities.

The band has invited guest rockers to accompany them and has worked with Bruce Springsteen, Judy Collins, and Warren Zevon. Robin Williams opened for them when they performed for Book Expo, the American Booksellers Association convention, in New York City in 1992.[9]

The band has toured the West Coast and even played The Rock and Roll Hall of Fame. But Dave Barry has said they "play music as well as Metallica writes novels."[10] Although members of the band teased one another about their skill as a band, they made plans for a 2007 midwestern bus tour.

Tan continued to publish while touring with the band. *The Moon Lady*, a picture book illustrated by Gretchen Shields, who also illustrated the covers of Tan's adult books, came out in 1992. This book tells the story of a child's travels to an autumn moon festival where she hopes to have the wishes of her heart granted by Lady Chang-o who lives on the moon. Lady Chang-o fulfills wishes once a year at the festival. The story won acclaim as "a story with deep, satisfying meanings, a tale of a lost child who for a prolonged and terrifying moment risks losing even her sense of self."[11]

Tan's second children's book, *Sagwa, The Chinese Siamese Cat*, was published in 1994.[12] Gretchen Shields illustrated this book also. In this original folktale, a Siamese cat tells her kittens

---

On *The Simpsons*

Perhaps because of their musical connection, Tan agreed with Matt Groening to star in an episode of *The Simpsons*. In a scene where Lisa Simpson goes to a book fair to meet her favorite authors, Lisa tells Tan that she loves the way Tan demystified mother-daughter relationships. Tan responds, "That's not what my books are about. Sit down. I'm ashamed for both of us."[13]

---

about their great ancestor, a mischievous white kitten who lives with her parents in the house of a greedy magistrate. Sagwa's adventures lead into one problem after another. After landing in a pot of ink, Sagwa emerges with the black markings of a Siamese cat, which leads to generations of Chinese cats with Siamese characteristics.[14]

Tan's creative world expanded once again when the Public Broadcasting System (PBS) opted to make this picture book into an animated children's television series called *Sagwa*. It has also been made into a symphony produced by George Daughtery.[15]

Chapter 6

The Hundred Secret Senses

Once again telling the story of a mother and daughter, Tan's third adult novel, *The Hundred Secret Senses*, is filled with ghosts and mysticism. Published in 1995, this novel traces the relationship of Olivia Bishop of half-Chinese and half-American descent, with her irresponsible mother. It also reveals the difficulties and resentments Olivia experiences with her relationship to her Chinese sister, Kwan. It does not help that Kwan sees Yin People and Olivia does not believe in this possibility. After the death of Olivia's father when she is only four, Kwan, twelve years Olivia's senior, arrived in the United States and becomes almost a mother substitute to Olivia. Olivia perceives Kwan as foolish, annoying, embarrassing, and a target for Olivia's abuse.

Shortly after her arrival in the United States, when Kwan holds conversations with Yin People, or ghosts, this lands her in a mental institution.

The novel opens with fully American Olivia, now thirty, still embarrassed by her sister. To complicate matters, Olivia is separating from her husband, Simon. Kwan convinces Olivia and Simon to travel with her to China. While Kwan makes efforts to reunite Olivia and Simon on this journey, a second narrative unfolds. It is Kwan's story of an earlier life. That story serves Kwan's efforts to open Olivia's eyes to a spiritual world, a world in which the World of Yin is real and reincarnation is the truth.[1]

While Tan considers herself a realistic and logical person, she admits *The Hundred Secret Senses*

Yin People

Luck is not simply a fluke said Tan, who believes that something, be it ghosts, God, or Yin People, brings her work into the right hands at the most appropriate place and time.[2] There are some things, Tan believes, that can not be rationally explained.

Tan herself has described incidents that include the knowledge of events before they happen, coincidence, prophetic dreams, and feelings that flood her brain with images, as supernatural reality. She told one interviewer, "My subconscious is open to the idea of something beyond the normal senses."[3]

came out of her own belief that the world includes invisible footsteps, prophetic dreams and daylight apparitions.[4]

Critics called this novel "enticing."[5] It is a story that reflects the reality of a supernatural world, a world in which the past and present collide to bring about personal understanding. In the case of *The Hundred Secret Senses*, misunderstanding is replaced with understanding only when Olivia accepts Kwan, their shared legacy, and the belief in the spirit world.[6]

Perhaps in an effort to share her own good fortune when this book came out, Tan became involved in efforts to raise money for educational and medical programs to help Chinese orphans through the Philip Harden Charitable Foundation. In March 1996, Tan returned to Beijing, China, to host and speak at a fund-raising banquet for this cause. More than four hundred people, including the U.S. ambassador John Sasser had paid seventy dollars a ticket to attend. Shortly before the guests arrived at the Beijing Holiday Inn Lido Hotel, police swarmed the facility in an effort to close down the event. According to a reporter, the charity had been confused with human-rights organizations that had criticized abuses at Chinese orphanages. After considerable negotiation, the police allowed the dinner to take place as long as everything that publicized the event was removed. Police pulled down banners and placards that read: "Love children," and "Help orphans." Although Tan's speech was canceled, she made a

Banned in China

Tan's fund-raising efforts for orphanages in China had a political impact that reached far beyond the original event Tan attended in Beijing in 1996. When she attempted to return to China, Tan was unable to get a visa to continue travel to research her adult novels or to visit relatives still living in Asia. While Tan was disheartened not to get into China, she was more concerned about the adoptions that might have been stalled or even stopped.[7]

She had originally became concerned about the welfare of children in China after seeing a documentary called *The Dying Room*, which drew the conclusion that many Chinese baby girls were being killed in Chinese orphanages. While the documentary drew outrage from many in the United States who wanted to help the children, it stalled adoptions to the United States. The Chinese government was so angry that, for a time, it even refused to take donations for orphan surgeries, such as cleft palates. The government's response to criticism of its practices would haunt Tan for years.[8]

point of going from table to table to tell each participant about the organization's efforts to help orphans.[9]

With each success, Tan became more aware of the way literary critics and academic writers viewed her work. She was always astonished that they found so much social, political, and cultural meaning in stories that she wrote simply to help her understand her own world and experiences.[10]

Much of the speculation about symbolism and author intention that academic writers placed on her works amused Tan, who said that sometimes the author is the last to know what she means when she writes. She commented, "The truth is, I do indeed include images in my work, but I don't think of them as symbols. . . . If there are symbols in my work, they exist largely by accident, or

---

On a CliffsNotes' Shelf

Tan enjoys the irony of discovering *The Joy Luck Club* had made it into CliffsNotes alongside William Shakespeare and a number of other classic authors. She recalled opening the yellow paperback readers' guide with amusement and curiosity. She was amazed that academics found so much relevance and meaning in stories she had considered simply stories to help her understand her own life. In the end, she said, to be shelved alongside dead authors made her feel that she was far from a classic author.[11]

STONY CREEK LIBRARY
1350 GREENFIELD PIKE
NOBLESVILLE, IN 46060

in someone else's interpretive design. . . . If I wrote of an orange moon rising on a dark night, I would more likely ask myself later if the image was clichéd, not whether is was a symbol of the feminine force rising in anger, as one master's thesis postulated."[12]

While others concluded that lessons could be drawn from Tan's books, their interpretations made her even more wary. Tan insisted that she had only wanted to tell a story. She had no intention of teaching lessons about being a Chinese American, about China, or about mothers and daughters.[13]

Chapter 7

Bittersweet Success

Tan believes her literary success can be summed up with a recurring dream she often had of making a phone call on a pay phone only to have the phone gobble up her change and go dead. Once her writing began producing sales and awards, the dream shifted so that money would pour from the change return.[1] But while her books provided fame and fortune, they could not save her from difficult times. Literary and financial success proved to be bittersweet when Tan realized that her mother's sudden inability to remember parts of her life was caused by Alzheimer's disease.

Tan continued working on her next novel, *The Bonesetter's Daughter*, while caring for her mother after the diagnosis. "Like a lot of caregivers, I went to support groups," Tan said of that time.

"We could talk about frustrations but also laugh about what the afflicted parent had done or said that was so off and yet so true."[2]

Tan also recognized that her life, despite her mother's failing health, was blessed in many ways. She had the financial means to get the best care for her mother, her family was close, and her friends enjoyed spending time with Tan and her mother.

During this period, Tan was invited to edit *The Best American Short Stories, 1999*. Guest editing might prove to be the best distraction, she thought. Tan was, in her own words, "having an awful time writing my fourth novel." Tan worried. "I worried that my bad writing might affect my reading," she wrote in the introduction to the collection. "Conversely, I worried that reading excellent stories would depress me and further undermine my writing."[3]

With the arrival of the first packet of more than forty short stories, Tan was taken back to the time in 1985 when reading short stories had been the springboard to writing her own stories. She set to work and over the course of the year, she read hundreds of stories. Tan found, in the end, that reading these short stories helped her writing immensely. "It sprang me out of the doldrums, and I had the same fervor and compulsion toward writing that I had had when I started reading massive amounts of fiction in 1985. By reading so many stories, so many voices, I unleashed what propelled me to write fiction in the first place: finding my own voice and telling my own story."[4]

Those stories might also have helped Tan to cope with her mother's failing health. Despite her mother's memory loss, Tan believes her mother had a full life up until the very end. "She adored being the center of attention," Tan said. "She also said in her last years words I never thought I'd hear: 'I'm happy. I have no worries.'"[5]

To help her through these days as a caretaker, Tan also relied on her writing. She told her friend Molly Giles, "Fiction helps you observe life and character. It is a jumping off point for thinking about your own life."[6]

Tan contemplated her writing after her mother's death on November 22, 1999.[7] At the time,

---

Her Mother Is Her Muse

After Daisy Tan's death, Tan said that if it were not for her mother, she would never have become a writer. "My mother said to me 20 years ago, during a moment when we weren't getting along well, 'If I die, what will you remember?' I realized I had no idea what I'd remember and what was important. My first book was in answer to her question." Tan added that her mother was really her muse. "She was someone who read fiction. She did not read most of my books. And yet she was my muse. The questions she had, the fact that she never felt that anything was impossible—what's in all of my books is the quality of hope that she had in her life."[8]

---

she said she hoped she could still communicate with her mother. "When I write," Tan explained, "it's such a meditative process. Ideas and images for stories come in unexpected ways—sometimes in remarkable ways that I can't explain. I often feel that I can't take credit. I'd like to think my mom will come and help me."[9]

But shortly after her mother's death, Tan's own health took a sudden turn.

She woke one day with a stiff neck, followed by bouts of insomnia and a constant headache. Her back hurt and then her shoulder froze. Tan passed these symptoms off to "too much airplane travel."[10]

Her symptoms worsened. "In 2000," she says, "I became really, really afraid. I felt there was darkness all around me. I had this sensation that there was always a knife aimed at my back. I couldn't leave the house by myself. I would check the doors. It was the constant presence of danger and the expectation that something terrible was about to happen."[11]

She was diagnosed with depression. Despite medication, her symptoms did not improve. She remained tired and jittery. Her feet grew numb. "Who was I to complain? I had a wonderful life, a great husband, lovely homes, a successful career."[12]

Although she managed to continue revision work on her next novel, *The Bonesetter's Daughter*, new writing came to a standstill when her symptoms worsened. Tan said, in one interview, that she really became worried when she started to hallucinate. Finally, she was unable to construct one sentence on a page. She began searching the Internet for causes and cures and was soon seeing specialists. "I certainly considered Alzheimer's, especially when I started having memory problems, and hiding mistakes that I'd made. I thought that this must have been what it was like for my mother," Tan said.[13]

She went from one specialist to another. She even consulted a psychiatrist. She researched her symptoms on the Web and finally realized that a tick bite at an outdoor wedding more than

---

What Is Lyme Disease?

Lyme disease is caused by a tick bite that usually leaves a bull's-eye rash, a red mark in the middle, circled by a pale ring which, in turn, is circled by a larger red ring. Early symptoms can include fever, fatigue, headache, and muscle and joint aches. If left untreated, patients with Lyme disease can experience sleep disturbances, fatigue, memory disorders, and even personality changes. Although the disease can be disabling, it is rarely fatal.

Lyme disease treatment usually consists of ten days of oral antibiotics. In extreme cases, some physicians recommend treatment with antibiotics for up to two years.[14]

---

four years before might have infected her with Lyme disease.[15]

She continued to research until she came across the name of a San Francisco Lyme specialist, Rafael Stricker. Tan learned she had late-stage neuroborreliosis and was put on a series of antibiotics. She was warned it could take months, even years to regain her health fully. But she was finally able to write again, and she knew she was on a path to recovery.[16]

Chapter 8

The Bonesetter's Daughter

Two weeks after the death of her mother, Tan's editor and friend, Faith Sales, died. Tan recalled, "I was suddenly faced with the loss of two people I loved and who had always protected me. Yet the experience of loss was also one of letting go of fears and uncertainties."[1]

Tan sat down to look at her manuscript of *The Bonesetter's Daughter* and revise it one last time. It turned into a major revision. In fact, Tan completely rewrote the novel from beginning to end. In many ways, the story reflects her mother's life and her own loss of that mother to Alzheimer's, but the novel is also about a young woman finding the truth of her mother's story by discovering that mother's secret life and reality.[2]

"I wanted the book to be about the discovery of our true names, our true pasts, our true natures," said Tan who felt the presence of both her mother and editor when she made these revisions.[3]

The Bonesetter's Daughter, published in 2001, is divided into three sections. The novel begins and ends in present-day California and tells the story of Ruth Young, a Chinese-American woman whose ten-year relationship with a man she loves becomes complicated when she realizes her mother is suffering dementia and needs her help. Ruth recognizes that, when her mother's stories disappear from her memory, Ruth will lose the chance to understand her family. The middle section of the novel is the memoir of LuLing, Ruth's mother, written to preserve the family's truth.[4]

When asked if she was writing about the loss of a parent's stories as a way to understand her own past, Tan said, "I had to be prodded by the fact that my mother was aging and I feared losing her." Tan explained that like most adolescents, she rejected her parents' pasts and, in doing so, she rejected their personal histories in her efforts to become an independent individual. "But then we discover the sub-layers of ourselves," she said, "and we realize we are shaped by our parents and personal history."[5]

As Ruth learns her mother's history, she recognizes her mother's strength. She discovers that to be a strong individual she needs connections between herself and her mother, and in her connections and relationships with others.

One reviewer, Nancy Willard, said that reading this novel "is like looking into a carved ivory ball that contains numerous smaller balls, each revealing a different design but all worked from a single source." According to Willard, "Tan's concern for what memory keeps and what it elects to hide is that single source."[6]

While Willard commented that the novel's theme reflects Tan's belief that silence can lead to misunderstandings, Tan allows Ruth to recognize that even when we speak or listen what we know of our relationships plays a role in misunderstandings. As Ruth comments, "There is always distortion between what a speaker says and what a listener wants it to mean."[7]

The Bonesetter's Daughter seems to capture Tan's intention to discover the truth of her own mother and daughter relationship through her writing. The novel portrays the dynamics of mothers and daughters in the way "the legacies of secrets that were kept too long create much of the tension between the novel's mothers and daughters." It mirrors the way Daisy Tan's secrets created tension between Tan and her mother.

Silence, of course, plays a part in keeping secrets. In the novel, Ruth loses her voice as a child, then again for short periods of time as an adult. Finally, Ruth chooses to remain silent for a few weeks annually. In LuLing's story, we learn that Precious Auntie, the nurse who in truth is

---

Reviews Go Unread

Some critics have criticized Tan's novels saying they tend to be a little bland and the themes of mothers and daughters caught up in misunderstandings can seem a bit repetitive. Despite many awards and the international success of the film *The Joy Luck Club*, they harped on Tan, saying her stories indicated she was "no intellectual." Tan stopped reading reviews of her work after one critic wrote that it was a big mistake for Tan to think her own life was so interesting others would want to read about it.[8]

LuLing's mother, lost the ability to speak as the result of an accident. In contrast, Tan wanted Ruth to use her silence with intent. "She *decided* to remain silent." Tan said, "Not speaking out of anger equals power. Women in my family haven't always had a voice. I wanted to give women a voice." Tan believes Ruth's decision to be silent is the way Ruth can finally find the power to be heard.[9]

The public grew used to seeing a book every few years from Tan. So, although she was recuperating from Lyme disease, she continued to work for short spurts of time until she would grow fatigued. But Tan realized that she could not put in the hours it would take to finish the next novel. Her editor suggested that Tan gather essays and articles she might have already published, speeches she might have given, and small vignettes from earlier musings. Her nonfiction collection *The Opposite of Fate: A Collection of Musings*, was published in 2003. The book was called "a breezy, readable book."[10]

The essays reflect the dramas in Tan's life. One essay that is also posted on her Web site corrects all the media misinformation about Tan. A few essays use humor to define Tan's difficult relationship with her mother. In one, Tan recalls her mother telling her never to kiss boys. "You do," Tan quotes her mother, "[t]hen you have baby. You put baby in garbage can. Police find you, put you in jail, then you life over, better just kill

A Collection That Reflects Fate and Faith

The Opposite of Fate, published in 2003, also turned out to be a collection of musings on the parallel roles that fate and faith have played in Tan's life. "It has to do with my upbringing with a father who very strongly believed in faith as a Baptist minister, and my mother, who very strongly believed in fate, and I'm trying to find things that work for me," Tan said of the collection.[11]

Part autobiography, part musings, Tan explained that the essays she chose describe the things that matter most to her. "I've only had one life and these are the aspects of my life that I continue to dwell upon."[12]

How the New York City skyline looked before the September 11, 2001, terrorist attacks on the World Trade Center, with the twin towers standing tall and proud.

yourself."[13] One of the final essays describes Tan's battle to discover what was wrong with her before she was diagnosed with Lyme disease.

While Tan toured to promote *The Opposite of Fate*, she was also making appearances for the Public Broadcasting Service's animated television series based on her children's book, *Sagwa, The Chinese Siamese Cat.*

During a scheduled appearance in the CNN news offices in New York City on September 11, 2001, Tan learned that two planes had hit the World Trade Center. Reporters scrambled to get the news on the air while she sat watching the monitors, thinking this must be the end of the world. "This was a momentous day for everybody," Tan said.[14]

Over the next few months, the events that played out served to change her thoughts about the way she lived. As government leaders claimed the United States needed to go to Afghanistan and then to war with Iraq, Tan asked herself, "What is my moral responsibility? What is my response?"[15]

As a writer and as an individual, she did not think morality could be legislated or passed down. She realized it comes out of questioning. After considering where moral decisions might come from, Tan concluded, "Morality is a very personal thing."[16]

Through her own musing on this topic, Tan realized she wanted her readers to question the truth. Morality became the theme for her next novel. But she also knew that she could not force

Honoring Her Mother
With Potstickers

The Opposite of Fate came out around the fourth anniversary of Daisy Tan's death, and Tan and her siblings paid tribute by making their mother's traditional Chinese dish, potstickers. Made of pan-fried pork dumplings, potstickers are golden and crisp. Tan's mother was renowned for hers. "We try to make potstickers and then we criticize the potstickers and say how bad they are," Tan told a reporter with the *San Francisco Chronicle* on that anniversary. The recipe has always been enjoyed throughout China by all classes. Tan concluded, "Anyone can enjoy them and everyone throughout China makes them. You can go to the most humble dwellings with outdoor kitchens and the wok resting on a pile of rocks and make them." Tan said her mother made potstickers for birthdays and every few weeks. "She would count on us eating 25 of them and she would make hundreds of these things. They were always our favorite meal."[17]

Amy Tan and her siblings paid tribute to their mother on the fourth anniversary of her death by making a traditional Chinese dish known as potstickers.

readers to be interested in a book that told them what to think or demanded that they question. She said, "My reasons for writing books are often not the reasons that you read the books."[18]

Tan decided to write to find out if bad intentions lead to good outcomes. She asked herself, can we take the credit? If we choose to do something good, but it turns out badly, are we responsible? Finally, she asked, "Is it important for us to have the credit?"[19]

Tan knew then that this book needed to be something different. She intended to write a funny novel, but not just a funny novel, one that might even be absurd.

Chapter 9

Saving Fish From Drowning

With ideas for another novel brewing, Tan's struggle to regain her health so she could write became more urgent. When her physicians decided to keep her on antibiotics for a few years, she found that, although she still had periods of pain and fatigue, she finally improved and gained strength.

Tan reflected that she had spent the past few years coping with debilitating disease within herself and her mother. She had watched her mother's mind slowly slip away. While there might have been a certain relief that her mother was no longer suffering, Tan mourned her mother terribly. Although Tan realized she was more upset about her mother's death than she would have expected, each passing day eased her grief.[1]

Finally, Tan believed she might be ready to tackle her next novel. But her mother had always been the narrative voice in her novels and Tan no longer had her mother at her side. When she wrote, Tan felt lost.

Tan said it might have been her imagination, or it might have been the spirit of her mother sitting on the edge of her bed. Whatever it was, her mother told Tan that she did not have to be a mother's voice. She could be anybody. She could even be a tour guide. In fact, she could even be a dead tour guide.[2]

With that realization, Tan embraced work on her next novel, *Saving Fish From Drowning*, with new energy and humor. Tan said, "My mother is nowhere or everywhere. She's freed from being a mother and she can be anything, and she's a tour guide."[3]

During a speech Tan made at a San Francisco bookstore, she explained that this was a very different book from all her others. Rather than focusing on mother and daughter relationships, this novel is about one of twelve people who journey to Burma, now known as Mynamar. The narrator is Bibi Chan, a dead tour guide, who has the ability to recognize the irony of people's intentions and knows the results of those intentions from the other side of life.[4]

This novel would explore the world of the spirit, but it also explored the consequences of good intentions. The narrator, herself a spirit, died brutally just before she was to lead a group of San

Francisco tourists on a sightseeing tour of Burma. The twelve travelers choose to embark on the tour despite Bibi's sudden death. They include five men, five women, and two children. During the course of their journey, the travelers fall in love and lust with one another. The travelers disappear on Christmas day, kidnapped by a tribe that mistakes one of the group for a political savior, a god called Younger White Brother.[5]

The travelers include Harry, a celebrity dog trainer who lusts after Marlena Chu, a professional art curator traveling with her daughter. Bibi's closest friend, Vera, is on the tour, along with a Darwin scholar and her husband, a bamboo grower and his sullen fifteen-year-old son, a wealthy left-wing activist, a psychologist, a woman who suffers from a myriad of vague symptoms, and an alternate tour director.[6]

While their behavior throughout the trip depicts their ignorance of other cultures, the group demonstrates a noble desire to help those less fortunate even while held captive by the tribe. Once they understand the tribe's needs, they even attempt to use their money to change the country's politics.

The novel's title reflects the Burmese reverence for all things living and the efforts to which fishermen will go in order to avoid bad karma.[7] When a fish is removed from the water and brought to shore, Burmese fishermen say they are saving the fish from drowning. As one of the guides observes, "Unfortunately, the fish do not recover."[8]

The fish story also serves as a metaphor for the way the tourists' good intentions do not always lead to positive consequences. "It was a wonderful metaphor for the questions of moral ambiguity and responsibility she wanted at the heart of the novel," said one book reviewer when the novel came out in 2005.[9]

Another reviewer said the book is a "superbly executed, goodhearted farce that is part romance and part mystery with a political bent."[10]

While the novel has been applauded for its humor, Tan pointed out this is also a novel of darkness. "It takes us to a place where we feel. It takes us to a very dark place, to this jungle," Tan said. "The dark places of our lives. To get to those dark places I think we have to be lured," Tan said, describing the way the tribal people lure the tourists to their hidden village.[11]

Tan chose Burma as the setting for this novel after she was offered the opportunity to travel there as part of an art expedition. While making her travel plans, Tan learned that writers are not allowed into Burma under the current government. She said, "I put on my visa that I was a consultant for a children's programme because I was working on a TV series based on a children's book of mine."[12]

The narrative spirit allowed Tan to create an omniscient or godlike perspective so that the reader experiences the humor and irony of well-intentioned people caught up in an unfamiliar culture.[13]

USA Today called the novel "a hilarious yet politically charged tale packed with illusions and the capacity for love." The reviewer concluded, "*Saving Fish From Drowning* succeeds because Tan combines humor, tragedy, politics, even a game of *Survival* Burma-style, without compromising a rollicking, adventure-filled story."[14]

Although this book is recognized for taking a huge leap away from stories of mothers and daughters, Tan said this book is based on the evolution of her own understanding of the way her relationship with her mother changed after her mother's death.

The Question of Beliefs

Although *Saving Fish From Drowning* is not one of Tan's more traditional mother–daughter novels, it does seek answers to questions that Tan admitted she has always asked: Where do these beliefs come from? How much of what an adult believes came from a mother's beliefs? A father's? How much of a person's beliefs come from rejecting parents' beliefs?

Tan said that *Saving Fish From Drowning* is about intentions and all the ways we look at the world. It is about the nature of beliefs. "Beliefs," she said, "govern intentions, intentions govern behavior."[15]

For Tan, "a mother brings *everything* into the realm of possibility."[16] Tan's mother loved to travel, and she loved to tell people about the places she had been. Hers is the voice of the dead tour guide in this book. As Bibi Chen, she recognizes that when people veer from a plan to pursue their own intentions—good or bad—conflict, confusion, and even chaos can result. In some ways, Bibi's is the voice of a mother who knows what's best. "In that sense, it is a mother-daughter story to me," explained Tan. "It's never going to be a mother-daughter story to anyone else. But, it's my mother-daughter story. My mother talking about things in the way she would have talked about them . . . her critical nature, her biases, and her regrets . . . all those things about her."[17]

If Tan was writing to understand, one question she asked in tackling this novel was how might individuals deal with the suffering of others. She told an interviewer, "I realize that at this point in my life, the things that I think about a lot have to do with discomfort, discomfort about what I feel about the suffering of people, of what I'm supposed to be doing, what I can do, what I can't do, what I don't want to do."[18]

Tan believed the tragedies in her own life taught her to empathize with others who suffer. There was the death of her father and brother, managing her mother's depression, the murder of a good friend, her mother's Alzheimer's and subsequent death, the death of her editor and friend

Faith Sales. She could not discount her own debilitating illness: Lyme disease. She said, "I think that until you physically suffer and feel helpless and hopeless and wonder who is going to help you and how . . . I think that was the turning point."[19]

During 2005, Tan turned her empathy into action once again. She began raising funds for victims of Hurricane Katrina. In concert with Writers4relief, a San Francisco group that included Maxine Hong Kingston, Dave Eggers, and Amistead Maupin among others, author readings helped raise more than forty thousand dollars. As part of the effort, Chronicle Books donated books for a relief auction.[20]

As fate would have it, even as Tan has taken time for charity, interest in Tan's work continued to take creative twists over the years. *Sagwa, The Chinese Siamese Cat* has maintained a long run as an animated television series. On occasion, Tan continues to join the San Francisco symphony to read the story in company to their music.

The San Francisco Theater has also staged, "The Immortal Heart," a chapter from *The Bonesetter's Daughter*. This play toured parts of the United States and was even staged in Paris.

Recently, Tan made another trip to China, this time to study Chinese musical instruments to be used in an opera based upon *The Bonesetter's Daughter*. Tan wrote the libretto, or the words, to the musical score composed by Stuart Wallace. This opera will be performed in English. "I first started this in ignorance," Tan said. "It was a much freer and more creative experience than I thought it could ever be."[21]

The opera's world premiere is scheduled for the San Francisco Opera's 2008–2009 season. Some of the scenes were successfully previewed by a small group of patrons in December 2006. Tan said the whole idea of the opera was born when a friend of hers asked Wallace to compose a song based on part of Tan's book for her birthday.[22]

She told the opera's audience that the novel's story "is about our family, but it is also about all families." Tan herself played the silent role of Precious Auntie, the character that in so many ways represents her own mother.[23]

Chapter 10

What Next?

While Tan continues to write, she also loves the creative challenges of adapting her writing to other media.

No matter what the medium, Tan said, "My hope is that every person is examining their own questions. My hope is that they realize the questions will change over our lives."[1]

Tan has not read reviews in years nor, for that matter, will she read anything that is written about her. "I would never be able to find anyone who represents me the way I see myself," she said. "We are all complex, fluid and full of conflicting views.[2]

She hopes that the teens who read her books are inspired by her questions. She suggested that those teens who wish to become writers recognize the importance of keeping journals. "I wish I had

Raising Funds for Kidney Transplants

Tan began co-chairing an annual authors' luncheon in San Francisco in efforts to raise awareness and funds for the National Kidney Foundation. Her interest in the organization came about quite awhile ago after she had an MRI that revealed she might possess three kidneys. A few years later, she learned she actually had only two kidneys.

The first luncheon that Tan hosted as an unknown writer drew four hundred people. By 2003, the luncheon drew 1,400 participants and raised $250,000 for the foundation's education and research programs.[3]

Amy Tan and husband Lou DeMattei attend the 2006 Champions of Hope Gala where Tan was being honored along with three others for their humanitarian work.

done this more—to write down in journals what I don't understand—what I hate, what I love—it would have to be sacred. I had a journal but I wasn't like that," she added.[4]

Tan continues to tour with the Rock Bottom Remainders. "I wear a blond wig now," she said.[5] She has also established herself nationally with a number of charities including The National Kidney Foundation and Lyme4Kids, a program to ensure that children are tested and treated for the disease. She continues to live in San Francisco with her husband, Lou DeMattei, and her two dogs, Bubba and Lilli.[6]

When she gives speeches or tours for a book, Tan travels with her two dogs who weigh between two and three pounds each. Lou DeMattei, Tan's husband, often travels to China with Tan and is himself on the board of Half the Sky, an organization formed to raise funds for Chinese orphans.[7]

Her dogs are her alarm clock, waking Tan and her husband up long before they are ready to be woken. "You have to wake up smiling and laughing," Tan said. "When the dogs are dancing on your chest and your face and your eyeballs, you're just laughing."[8]

Over the next years, Tan found herself a busy writer, editor, and humanitarian. In January 2006, Tan agreed to solicit fiction for the *Los Angeles Times'* Sunday magazine, *West*, as the literary editor.[9] Another novel, as yet untitled, is scheduled for 2009 publication.[10]

Each day finds Tan working on her writing, though. She takes on issues of love and hope. "What is important for me is to ask a lot of questions knowing I'm never going to find the answers," Tan said. "A lot of it comes from emotional need."[11]

She does not talk about what she is currently working on because she believes it loses energy. But it would not surprise any of Tan's readers if her mother's voice appeared again. "I love my mother's voice as a narrator because she's very open to so many things, she's open to God, reincarnation, magic, spirits. Her beliefs are inconsistent."[12]

It is those inconsistent beliefs that Tan has always found so fascinating. "We have to find what's meaningful," she said, adding, "The spirit is very personal to me."[13]

As she continues forward, Tan admits she has no real writing rituals, although she writes her first draft in longhand and only relies upon the computer to revise. She said she can write just about anywhere out of necessity, from hotel rooms to her bed, to her office in her house. "I put headphones on to block out noise."[14]

"These days I check my email and then I start writing," she said. If she has any process, it centers on the questions she asks. "You're juggling a lot of things," she explained about writing. "You have to think about what the question is that you're trying to answer for yourself."[15]

Amy Tan poses with a Yorkshire terrier during the American Film Institute (AFI) Fest 2007. She appears in the film *Hollywood Chinese*, a documentary about how the Chinese are portrayed in American cinema.

Tan acknowledged that writing is hard work, requiring focus, research, and revision. She loves this about writing. She said, "Hard work is good work."[16]

Sometimes, Tan has to stop and remind herself that people will be reading what she writes, and they will need to see it in the form of a story. She throws away hundreds of pages before she finds her focus. "The best is probably the last fifty pages of writing it. Then I know more what my focus is and I write much more quickly toward the end."[17]

Tan suspects that, no matter where her novels and other creative projects take her, she will always be known for her very first book. "I accept that probably for the rest of my life I will be identified with *The Joy Luck Club*—I will always be introduced as the author of *The Joy Luck Club*. On my tombstone, if I wanted a tombstone, which I don't—it would say Author of *The Joy Luck Club*. That's fine. I hope that I continue to write my best book with each book that I write. I am very lucky that that happened to me."[18]

In Her Own Words

The following section draws from a personal interview with Amy Tan conducted by the author on October 31, 2006, along with several other print and Web resources.

On Writing

"I believe that a writer does have to think about the responsibilities, but make them individually and never have them dictated to him or her. I think about the reasons I write and I have to be true to them. I want to write about how I've evolved as a person through the history of my family, or I want to write about the things that I believe and act them out in the way of a narrative."[1]

"Each book I write succeeds in ways aesthetically that I did not expect. Each book also fails in ways I would have hoped it would not. I think most writers are compelled in part to continue writing because we are trying to come closer to what our work of art should be. For me, language and a seamless and deceptively simple quality to the story are hugely important."[2]

"Fiction has a huge role in presenting the truth of anything—not the facts, but the feelings, what you feel, what others feel, what your moral position is, your version of the truth."[3]

"When I begin a novel, I don't know where it will take me. I can't start with an answer, a pre-made conclusion that I then drive into place with the hammer of my words."[4]

"As a writer, I know that the expectations of a reader must be fulfilled. The loose ends have to be addressed, although not neatly and falsely tied into a dimensionality by the end. They are imperfect, yet they are loveable. Good that does no good is a disturbing notion. But what is a novel for it not to be provocative? Some stories exist to delve into questions that we don't want to ask."[5]

"I didn't write any of my books to help people understand but to find my own understanding."[6]

"I didn't write any of my books to help people understand their own lives better. If I'm honest, about my need to understand, I have to trust that the need will connect to a lot of people."[7]

"The hard work of writing is emotional, feeling insecure, feeling stupid. There's a fear that if things don't come out right, it will be wasted effort."[8]

"Focus is very hard work in this remote control age. To write a novel you have to remain extremely focused. There are so many details you need to keep in your head."[9]

"Start writing down in a journal what you feel about things. Write down the reasons you want to write even if you never get published. Just write. Be willing to revise. It's a craft."[10]

On Reading

"I loved fairy tales as a kid. Grim. The grimmer the better. I loved gruesome gothic tales, and, in that respect, I liked Bible stories, because to me they were very gothic."[11]

"I am a voracious reader. . . . I never turn on the television."[12]

"Certainly *Jane Eyre* fits in there with the bests."[13]

"To this day, I love reading dictionaries, including lexicons of dead languages. I love the sounds and shapes of words, the way certain consonant blends can evoke related images: *glow, glisten, glimmer, glen*. . . ."[14]

"If a daughter feels ugly, a daughter's not going to hear her mother when she says, 'You're beautiful.' Maybe it's better to read a story that is related to what she's going through."[15]

"Maybe it's a good idea for mothers and daughters to read the same book together rather than for mothers to protect or tell their daughters how to behave or feel."[16]

"I'm reading *Ada or Ardor: A Family Chronicle* right now. It's not an easy book to read. I tried once before. All the parenthetical intrusions were difficult to ignore. Now I'm at a place in life where I often create parenthetical thought in my own speech so I relate."[17]

Chronology

1913—John Tan, Amy Tan's father, is born.

1916—Du Ching or Daisy, Amy Tan's mother, is born.

1941—Daisy and John meet.

1945—Daisy and John are together briefly in China.

1949—Daisy comes to the United States to marry John.

1950—Peter Tan is born.

1952—Amy Tan is born on February 19.

1967—Peter Tan dies of a brain tumor on July 1.

1968—John Tan does of a brain tumor on February 5.

1972—Amy Tan graduates from San Jose State University as an honor student with a BA, double majoring in linguistics and English.

1974—Tan and Lou DeMattei marry.

1989—*The Joy Luck Club* is published in March and is named a National Book Award Finalist in November.

1991—*The Kitchen God's Wife* is published; Tan joins the Rock Bottom Remainders.

1992—Filming of *The Joy Luck Club* begins.

1993—The film *The Joy Luck Club* is released.

1994—*Sagwa, The Chinese Siamese Cat* is published. PBS turns it into a children's animated series.

1995—*The Hundred Secret Senses* is published.

1996—Tan raises funds for the Philip Harden Charitable Foundation to be used for Chinese orphans; Tan is denied a visa to travel to China for research.

1999—Tan edits *The Best American Short Stories, 1999*; Tan's mother Daisy Tan dies on November 22; Faith Sales, Tan's editor and friend, dies on December 7.

2001—*The Bonesetter's Daughter* is published; Tan is in the CNN offices in New York City when the World Trade Center is hit by planes piloted by terrorists on September 11.

2003—*The Opposite of Fate* is published.

2005—*Saving Fish from Drowning* is published.

2006—*The Immortal Heart*, a play based upon *The Bonesetter's Daughter*, is staged in San Francisco before it tours the country and finally closes in Paris, France. Scenes from the opera based upon *The Bonesetter's Daughter* are performed at the San Francisco Opera.

2008—The opera, *The Bonesetter's Daughter*, is debuted at the San Francisco Opera.

2009—Tan's most recent novel (no title yet) will debut.

Selected Works of Amy Tan

Novels

1989   *The Joy Luck Club*

1991   *The Kitchen God's Wife*

1992   *The Moon Lady*

1994   *Sagwa, The Chinese Siamese Cat*

1995   *The Hundred Secret Senses*

2001   *The Bonesetter's Daughter*

2005   *Saving Fish from Drowning*

Collections

1999   *Contributing editor, Best American Short Stories*

Short Stories and Articles

1988   *PM Five,* "End Game"

           Seventeen, "End Game"

1989   *Glamour,* "Watching China"

1990   *The State of Language,* "The Language of Discretion"

1991   *Life,* "Lost Lives of Women"

1996   *Harper's,* "In the Canon, For All the Wrong Reasons"

Nonfiction

2003   *The Opposite of Fate*

Films

The Joy Luck Club—co-screenwriter with Ron
    Bass and coproducer with Wayne Wang.

Introductions and Forewords by Amy Tan

Bei, Ai, translated by Howard Goldblatt. *Red Ivy,
    Green Earth Mother*. iUniverse,
    Incorporated, 2000.

Bowen, Richard, and Karin Evans. *Mei Mei—
    Little Sister: Portraits From a Chinese
    Orphanage*. San Francisco, Calif.:
    Chronicle Books LLC, 2005.

Foo, Susanna. *Susanna Foo Chinese Cuisine: The
    Fabulous Flavors and Innovative Recipes of
    North America's Finest Chinese Cook*. New
    York: Houghton Mifflin, 2002.

Pottruck, Emily Scott. *Tails of Devotion: A Look at
    the Bond Between People and Their Pets*.
    San Francisco, Calif.: Tails of Devotion,
    2005.

Opera

2008   *The Bonesetter's Daughter*

Plays

2006   *The Immortal Heart*

Television

2001-2002   *Sagwa, The Chinese Siamese Cat*

Symphony

2001   *Sagwa, The Chinese Siamese Cat*

Awards

The Joy Luck Club

New York Times best-seller list – 40 weeks

National Book Award Finalist

The National Book Critics Circle Award Finalist

Bay Area Book Reviewers Award

Commonwealth Gold Award

Los Angeles Times Fiction Prize Finalist

American Library Association's Notable Books

American Library Association's Best Book for Young Adults

Selected for the National Endowment for the Art's Big Read

The Kitchen God's Wife

New York Times Notable Book

American Library Association Notable Book

Booklist Editor's Choice

The Hundred Secret Senses

Orange Prize Finalist

The Bonesetter's Daughter
>
> Orange Prize nomination
>
> *New York Times* Notable Book
>
> IMPAC Dublin Award nomination

The Opposite of Fate
>
> *New York Times* Notable Book
>
> Audie Award: Best Non-fiction, Abridged
>
> *Booklist* Editor's Choice

Saving Fish from Drowning
>
> *IMPAC* Dublin Award nomination
>
> *Booklist* Editor's Choice

Sagwa, animated series for PBS
>
> Emmy Award
>
> Parent Choice, Best Television Program for Children

The Joy Luck Club, film
>
> Shortlisted BAFTA Film Award, best screenplay adaptation
>
> Shortlisted WGA Award, best screenplay adaptation

Chapter Notes

Chapter 1. The Sleepy Therapist

1. Amy Tan, "Biography," *Amy Tan*, n.d., <http://www.amytan.net/ATBiography.aspx> (January 8, 2008).

2. Alden Mudge, "Short Story Master Tackles the Terrain of the Novel," *BookPage*, August 2000, <http://www.bookpage.com/0008bp/molly_giles.html> (January 8, 2008).

3. Ibid.

4. "Newsmakers," *First Monday*, San Francisco State University, March 5, 2001.

5. Angela Miyuki Mackintosh, "How Amy Tan Saved Me From Drowning," *WOW! Women on Writing*, December 2006, <http://wow-womenonwriting.com/4-amytan.php> (January 8, 2008).

6. "Newsmakers."

7. "Amy Tan: Bio," *Bookreporter.com*, n.d., <http://www.bookreporter.com/authors/au-tan-amy.asp> (January 8, 2008).

8. Amy Tan, e-mail message to author, January 23, 2007.

9. Amy Tan, "A Question of Fate," *The Opposite of Fate* (New York: G. P. Putnam and Sons, 2003), p. 54.

10. Ibid., p. 58.

11. Ibid., p. 59.

Chapter 2. From China to the United States

1. Amy Tan, "The CliffsNotes Version of My Life," *The Opposite of Fate* (New York: G. P. Putnam and Sons, 2003), p. 16.

2. Amy Tan, "My Grandmother's Choice," *The Opposite of Fate*, p. 102.

3. Ibid., p. 104.

4. Ibid., p. 102.

5. "Books: Author Profile: Amy Tan," *NDTV.com*, n.d., <http://www.ndtv.com/ent/booksprofiles.asp?id=18&author=Amy+Tan> (January 8, 2008).

6. Amy Tan, "What She Meant," *The Opposite of Fate*, p. 208.

7. Tan, "The CliffsNotes Version of My Life," p. 17.

8. Amy Tan, "Pretty Beyond Belief," *The Opposite of Fate*, pp. 215–217.

9. Tan, "The CliffsNotes Version of My Life," p. 14.

10. Ibid.

11. Amy Tan, e-mail message to author, January 23, 2007.

12. Tan, "The CliffsNotes Version of My Life," pp. 19–25.

13. Amy Tan, *Book Passage* speech, *FORA.tv*, November 7, 2006, <http://fora.tv/> (January 9, 2008).

14. Amy Tan, e-mail message to author, January 23, 2007.

15. "A Uniquely Personal Storyteller," *Academy of Achievement*, June 28, 1996, last updated October 22, 2006, <http://www.achieve-ment.org/autodoc/page/tan0int-1> (January 9, 2008).

16. Amy Tan, "Last Week," *The Opposite of Fate*, pp. 69–74.

17. "A Uniquely Personal Storyteller."

18. Amy Tan, "What the Library Means to Me," *The Opposite of Fate*, pp. 269–270.

19. "A Uniquely Personal Storyteller."

20. Ibid.

21. Ibid.

22. Ibid.

23. Donna Longenecker, "Relationship With Mother Helped Tan Hone Writing Skills." *University at Buffalo Reporter*, vol. 34, no. 18, March 27, 2003, <http://www.buffalo. edu/reporter/vol34/vol34n18/articles/AmyT an.html> (January 9, 2008).

24. Personal interview with Amy Tan, October 31, 2006.

25. Amy Tan, "Confessions," *The Opposite of Fate*, p. 213.

26. Personal interview with Amy Tan, October 31, 2006.

27. Amy Tan, "My Love Affair with Vladimir Nabokov," *The Opposite of Fate*, p. 223.

28. Tan, "Confessions," p. 212.

29. Tan, "My Love Affair With Vladimir Nabokov," pp. 221–222.

30. Tan, "The CliffsNotes Version of My Life," p. 30.

31. Amy Tan, "The Most Hateful Words," *The Opposite of Fate*, pp. 218–220.

32. Tan, "Confessions," pp. 212–213.

33. Personal interview with Amy Tan, October 31, 2006.

34. Ibid.

35. Tan, "The Most Hateful Words," p. 218.

36. Personal interview with Amy Tan, October 31, 2006.

37. Ibid.

38. Ibid.

39. Amy Tan, "Biography," *Amy Tan*, n.d., <http://www.amytan.net/ATBiography.aspx> (January 8, 2008).

40. Tan, "The CliffsNotes Version of My Life," p. 33.

41. Personal interview with Amy Tan, October 31, 2006.

Chapter 3. Finding Stories in *The Joy Luck Club*

1. Amy Tan, "The CliffsNotes Version of My Life," *The Opposite of Fate* (New York: G. P. Putnam and Sons, 2003), p. 33.

2. "Lou DeMattei," *Half the Sky Foundation*, n.d., <http://www.halfthesky.org/about/board.php> (January 10, 2008).

3. Amy Tan, "Biography," *Amy Tan*, n.d., <http://www.amytan.net/ATBiography.aspx> (January 8, 2008).

4. Amy Tan, "Q&A: A Discussion With *Amy Tan*," Amy Tan, n.d., <http://www.amytan.net/InterviewWithAmyTan.aspx> (January 9, 2008).

5. "Amy Tan: Bio," *Bookreporter.com*, n.d., <http://www.bookreporter.com/authors/ au-tan-amy.asp> (January 8, 2008).

6. Amy Tan, *Book Passage* speech, *FORA.tv*, November 7, 2006, <http://fora.tv/> (January 9, 2008).

7. Ibid.

8. Ibid.

9. Angela Miyuki Mackintosh, "How Amy Tan Saved Me From Drowning," *WOW! Women on Writing*, December 2006, <http://wow-womenonwriting.com/4-amytan.php> (January 8, 2008).

10. Ibid.

11. Ibid.

12. Sylvia Rubin, "Amy Tan's Got a New Attitude, Out of a Black Period, S.F. Writer Has New Book," *San Francisco Chronicle*, October 13, 1995, <http://sfgate.com/cgi-bin/article.cgi?file=/c/a/1995/10/13/DD7 0674.DTL> (January 9, 2008).

13. Julie Lew, "How Stories Written for Mother Became Amy Tan's Best Seller," *The New York Times*, July 4, 1989, <http://www.nytimes. com/books/01/02/18/specials/tan-seller. html> (January 30, 2008).

14. Mackintosh.

15. Ibid.

16. Lew.

17. Orville Schell, "Your Mother Is in Your Bones," *The New York Times*, March 19, 1989, <http://www.nytimes.com/books/01/02/18/specials/tan-joy.html> (January 30, 2008).

18. Amy Tan, *The Joy Luck Club* (New York: Ivy Books, 1989), pp. 3–4.

19. Amy Tan, Heggepin County Library Speaking Engagement, Minneapolis, October 2006.

20. Mackintosh.

21. Amy Tan, "What She Meant," *The Opposite of Fate*, p. 180.

22. Mackintosh.

23. Amy Tan, "Joy Luck and Hollywood," *The Opposite of Fate*, pp. 180–183.

24. Mackintosh.

25. Tan, "Joy Luck and Hollywood," p. 195.

26. Ibid., p. 197.

27. Ibid., p. 202.

28. Tan, "What She Meant," pp. 210–211.

29. Eden Ross Lipson, "The Wicked English-Speaking Daughter," *The New York Times*, March 19, 1989,<http://www.nytimes.com/books.01/02/18/specials/tan-joy.html> (February 13, 2008).

30. "Hillary Clinton's Bookshelf," *O, The Oprah Magazine*, July/August 2000, <http://www.oprah.com/obc/omag/bookshelf/omag_books_hillary_g.jhtml> (January 9, 2008).

Chapter 4. *The Kitchen God's Wife*

1. Mervyn Rothstein, "A New Novel by Amy Tan Who's Still trying to Adapt to Success," *The New York Times*, June 11, 1991, p. 2, <http://query.nytimes.com/gst/fullpage.html?res= 9DOCE5DD163AF932A25755COA96 7958260> (January 9, 2008).

2. Sylvia Rubin, "Amy Tan's Got a New Attitude, Out of a Black Period, S.F. Writer Has New Book," *San Francisco Chronicle*, October 13, 1995, <http://sfgate.com/cgi-bin/article.cgi?file=/c/a/1995/10/13/DD7 0674.DTL> (January 9, 2008).

3. Rothstein, p. 2.

4. Rubin.

5. Amy Tan, "Angst and the Second Book," *The Opposite of Fate* (New York: G. P. Putnam and Sons, 2003), pp. 330–331.

6. Ibid., p. 330.

7. Rothstein, pp. 2–3.

8. Sarah Lyall, "At Home With Amy Tan: In the Country of the Spirits," *The New York Times*, December 28, 1995, <http://www.nytimes. com/books/01/02/18/specials/tan-home.html> (February 5, 2008).

9. Ibid.

10. "All About Her Mother," *Guardian Unlimited*, December 5, 2005, <http://books.guardian. co.uk/departments/generalfiction/story/0,,1 657788,00.html> (January 30, 2008).

11. Rothstein, p. 1.

12. Robb Forman Dew, "Pangs of an Abandoned Child," *The New York Times*, June 16, 1991, <http://query.nytimes.com/gst/fullpage.html ?res=9D0CEFDE1038F935A25755C0A9 67958260> (January 9, 2008).

13. Rothstein, p. 2.

14. Xie Heng, "The Changing Role and Status of Women in China," *The 1900 Institute*, February 1994, <http://www.1990insti-tute.org/publications/pubs/ISUPAP8.html> (January 9, 2008).

15. Dorinda Elliott, "More Rights—At a Cost," *Newsweek*, 1998, <http://www.washington-post.com/wp-srv/newsweek/women.htm> (January 9, 2008).

16. Jami Edwards, "Interview," *Bookreporter.com*, n.d., <http://www.bookreporter.com/authors /au-tan-amy.asp> (January 9, 2008).

17. Rubin.

18. Ibid.

19. Ibid.

Chapter 5. A Band of Bookmakers

1. Amy Tan, "Midlife Confidential," *The Opposite of Fate* (New York: G. P. Putnam and Sons, 2003), pp. 138–139, 150–151.

2. Ibid., p. 139.

3. Ibid., pp. 150–153.

4. Amy Tan, "Biography," *Amy Tan*, n.d., <http://www.amytan.net/ATBiography.aspx> (January 8, 2008).

5. "Still Younger Than Keith Tour," The Rock Bottom Remainders Web site, n.d., <http://www.rockbottomremainders.com/pages/tour.html> (January 9, 2008).

6. Natchez Staff, "Natchez Author Joins Rock and Roll Band of Literary Giants," *The Natchez Democrat*, September 17, 2003, <http://www.natchezdemocrat.com/news/2003/sep/17/natchez-author-joins-rock-and-roll-band-of/> (February 13, 2008).

7. "About the Band Members," The Rock Bottom Remainders Web site, n.d., <http://www.rockbottomremainders.com/pages/about_the_band.html> (February 26, 2008).

8. "Natchez Author Joins Rock and Roll Band."

9. Amy Tan, *Book Passage* speech, *FORA.tv*, November 7, 2006, <http://fora.tv/> (January 9, 2008).

10. "Natchez Author Joins Rock and Roll Band."

11. Ellen Schecter, "Children's Books; Girl Overboard," *The New York Times*, November 8, 1992, <http://www.nytimes.com/books/01/02/18/specials/tan-moon.html> (February 13, 2008).

12. Tan, "Biography."

13. "All About Her Mother," *Guardian Unlimited*, December 5, 2005, <http://books.guardian.co.uk/departments/generalfiction/story/0,,1657788,00.html> (January 30, 2008).

14. Margaret A. Chang, Review of *Sagwa, The Chinese Siamese Cat* from the *School Library Journal*, 1994, *Amazon.com*, n.d., <http://www.amazon.com/Sagwa-Chinese-Siamese-Cat-Amy/dp/0689846177> (January 9, 2008).

15. Tan, "Biography."

Chapter 6. *The Hundred Secret Senses*

1. Claire Messud, "Ghost Story," *The New York Times*, October 29, 1995, <www.nytimes.com/books/01/02/18/specials/tan-hundred.html> (February 5, 2008).

2. Jami Edwards, "Interview," *Bookreporter.com*, n.d., <http://www.bookreporter.com/authors/au-tan-amy.asp> (January 9, 2008).

3. Sarah Lyall, "At Home With Amy Tan: In the Country of the Spirits," *The New York Times*, December 28, 1995, <http://www.nytimes.com/books/01/02/18/specials/tan-home.html> (February 5, 2008).

4. Edwards.

5. Messud.

6. Lyall.

7. Edwards.

8. "Author Talk," *Bookreporter.com*, November 2005, <http://www.bookreporter.com/authors/au-tan/asp> (February 13, 2008).

9. Rod Mickleburgh, "China Abruptly Halts Benefit for Orphans, S.F. Author Amy Tan Was to Be Featured Speaker at Beijing Dinner," *San Francisco Chronicle*, April 1, 1996, <http://www.sfgate.com/cgi-bin/article.cgi?file=/e/a/1996/04/01/NEWS6378.dtl> (January 9, 2008).

10. Edwards.

11. Amy Tan, *The Opposite of Fate* (New York: G. P. Putnam and Sons, 2003), p. 10.

12. Patricia Holt, "Between the Lines—Students Read a Lot Into Amy Tan," *San Francisco Chronicle*, August 18, 1996, <http://www.sfgate.com/cgi-bin/article.cgi?file=/chronicle/archive/1996/08/18/RV69717.DTL> (February 13, 2008).

13. Ibid.

Chapter 7. Bittersweet Success

1. Sarah Lyall, "At Home With Amy Tan: In the Country of the Spirits," *The New York Times*, December 28, 1995, <http://www.nytimes.com/books/01/02/18/specials/tan-home.html> (February 5, 2008).

2. Molly Giles, "Author Q & A," *The Bonesetter's Daughter*, Random House, Inc., n.d., <http://www.randomhouse.com/catalog/display.pperl?isbn=9780345457370&view=aqua> (September 19, 2006).

3. Amy Tan, "Introduction," *The Best American Short Stories 1999*, Katrina Kenison, ed. (New York: Houghton Mifflin and Company, 1999), p. xxiii.

4. Ibid., pp. xxiiv–xxv.

5. Giles.

6. Ibid.

7. Jonathan Curiel, "Mother of 'Joy Luck Club' Author Amy Tan Is Dead," San Francisco Chronicle, November 24, 1999, <http://www.sfgate.com/cgi-bin/ article.cgi?file=/c/a/1999/11/24/ MN68927.DTL> (January 9, 2008).

8. Ibid.

9. Ibid.

10. Amy Tan, "Amy Tan on Lyme Disease," *Amy Tan*, n.d., <http://amytan.net/LymeDisease. aspx> (January 9, 2008).

11. "All About Her Mother," *Guardian Unlimited*, December 5, 2005, <http://books.guardian. co.uk/departments/generalfiction/story/0,,1 657788,00.html> (January 30, 2008).

12. Tan, "Amy Tan on Lyme Disease."

13. JJ McCoy, "Novelist Lives Dramatic Struggle With Lyme Disease," *The Washington Post, Modbee.com*, August 13, 2003, <http:// www.modbee.com/life/healthyliving/story/72 81736p-820735c.html> (September 19, 2006).

14. McCoy.

15. "All About Her Mother."

16. McCoy.

Chapter 8. *The Bonesetter's Daughter*

1. Molly Giles, "Author Q & A," *The Bonesetter's Daughter*, Random House, Inc., n.d. <http://www.randomhouse.com/catalog/display.pperl?isbn=9780345457370&view=aqua> (September 19, 2006).

2. Amy Tan, *The Opposite of Fate* (New York: G. P. Putnam and Sons, 2003), pp. 96–97.

3. Giles.

4. Amy Tan, *The Bonesetter's Daughter* (New York: Ballentine Books, 2001).

5. Personal interview with Amy Tan, October 31, 2006.

6. Nancy Willlard, "Talking to Ghosts," *The New York Times*, February 18, 2001, <http://www.nytimes.com/books/01/02/18/reviews/010218.18williar.html> (February 5, 2008).

7. Tan, *The Bonesetter's Daughter*, p. 24.

8. "All About Her Mother," *Guardian Unlimited*, December 5, 2005, <http://books.guardian.co.uk/departments/generalfiction/story/0,,1657788,00.html> (January 30, 2008).

9. Personal interview with Amy Tan, October 31, 2006.

10. Clea Simon, "Amy Tan Explores the Interweaving of Fate, Fact and Fiction. Tan Takes a Look at Her Work, Life," *San Francisco Chronicle*, December 7, 2003, <http://www.sfgate.com/cgibin/article.cgi?file=/c/a/2003/12/07/RVGTV3BFNF1.DTL> (January 9, 2008).

11. Jay McDonald, "A Date With Fate: Tan's Memoir Probes Cosmic Connections," *BookPage*, November 2003, <http://www.bookpage.com/0311bp/amy_tan.html> (September 19, 2006).

12. Ibid.

13. Simon.

14. Amy Tan, *Book Passage* speech, *FORA.tv*, November 7, 2006, <http://fora.tv/> (January 9, 2008).

15. Ibid.

16. Ibid.

17. Bill Daley, "Potstickers in One Small Package, These Dumplings Link Past to Present, Rich to Poor, Mother to Daughter," *San Francisco Chronicle*, November 5, 2003, <http://www.sfgate.com/cgi-bin/article.cgi?file=/c/a/2003/11/05/FDGDV2LVGR1.DTL> (January 9, 2008).

18. Amy Tan, *Book Passage* speech.

19. Ibid.

Chapter 9. *Saving Fish From Drowning*

1. Amy Tan, *Book Passage* speech, *FORA.tv*, November 7, 2006, <http://fora.tv/> (January 9, 2008).

2. Ibid.

3. Angela Miyuki Mackintosh, "How Amy Tan Saved Me From Drowning," *WOW! Women on Writing*, December 2006, <http://wow-womenonwriting.com/4-amytan.php> (January 8, 2008).

4. Carol Memmott, "Tan's 'Fish' Will Hook Readers," *USA Today*, November 1, 2005, p. D4.

5. Sara Peyton, "A Ghost Goes to Burma in Tan's Latest," *San Francisco Chronicle*, October 30, 2005, <http://www.sfgate. com/cgibin/article.cgi?f=/c/a/2005/10/30/ RVGSOFBS G21.DTL> (February 13, 2008).

6. Ibid.

7. "All About Her Mother," *Guardian Unlimited*, December 5, 2005, <http://books.guardian. co.uk/departments/generalfiction/story/0,,1 657788,00.html> (January 30, 2008).

8. Memmott.

9. "All About Her Mother."

10. Peyton.

11. Personal interview with Amy Tan, October 31, 2006.

12. "All About Her Mother."

13. Amy Tan, *Saving Fish From Drowning* (New York: G. P. Putnam's Sons, 2005).

14. Memmott.

15. Tan, *Book Passage* speech, *FORA.tv*.

16. Ibid.

17. Mackintosh.

18. Rhonda Shafner, "Novelist Talks About Suffering of Others, and Her Own," *The Irrawaddy*, January 3, 2007, <http:// lymeblog.com/modules.php?name=News&file = article&sid=302> (February 5, 2008).

19. Ibid.

20. "Pics of the Week," *Publishers Weekly*, September 12, 2005, <http://www.publishersweekly.com/article/CA6261392.html> (February 5, 2008).

21. Tan, Book Passage speech, *FORA.tv*.

22. David Wiegand, "For a Privileged Few, a Sneak Preview of How an Opera Is Born," *San Francisco Chronicle*, December 6, 2006, <http://www.sfgate.com/cgi-bin/article.cgi?file=/c/a/2006/12/06/DDGBUMPP-SA1.DTL> (January 9, 2008).

23. Ibid.

Chapter 10. What's Next?

1. Personal interview with Amy Tan, October 31, 2006.

2. Ibid.

3. Catherine Bigelow, "Writers Crack Jokes Over Kidney Pains at Benefit," *San Francisco Chronicle*, December 14, 2003, <http://www.sfgate.com/cgi-bin/article.cgi?ffile=/c/a/2003/ 12/14/VGR33KILI1.DTL> (January 9, 2008).

4. Personal interview with Amy Tan, October 31, 2006.

5. Ibid.

6. Amy Tan, "Biography," *Amy Tan*, n.d., <http://amytan.net/ATBiography.aspx> (January 8, 2008).

7. "Lou DeMattei," *Half the Sky Foundation*, n.d., <http://www.halfthesky.org/about/board.php> (January 10, 2008).

8. Amy Tan, *Book Passage* speech, *FORA.tv*, November 7, 2006, <http://fora.tv/> (January 9, 2008).

9. "Amy Tan Named Literary Editor of New L.A. Times' Magazine," *USA Today*, January 13, 2006, <http://www.usatoday.com/life/people/2006-01-13-tan-editor_x.htm> (February 11, 2008).

10. Personal interview with Amy Tan, October 31, 2006.

11. Tan, *Book Passage* speech, *FORA.tv*.

12. Personal interview with Amy Tan, October 31, 2006.

13. Ibid.

14. Ibid.

15. Tan, *Book Passage* speech, *FORA.tv*.

16. Personal interview with Amy Tan, October 31, 2006.

17. Tan, *Book Passage* speech, *FORA.tv*.

18. "All About Her Mother," *Guardian Unlimited*, December 5, 2005, <http://books.guardian.co.uk/departments/generalfiction/story/0,,1657788,00.html> (January 30, 2008).

In Her Own Words

1. "Interview," *Bookreporter.com*, March 2001, <http://www.bookreporter.com/authors/au-tan-amy.asp> (February 13, 2008).

2. Jami Edwards, "Interview," *Bookreporter.com*, n.d., <http://www.bookreporter.com/authors/au-tan-amy.asp> (February 13, 2008).

3. "Author Talk," *Bookreporter.com*, November 2005, <http://www.bookreporter.com/authors/au-tan-amy.asp> (February 13, 2008).

4. Ibid.

5. Ibid.

6. Personal interview with Amy Tan, October 31, 2006.

7. Ibid.

8. Ibid.

9. Ibid.

10. Ibid.

11. "A Uniquely Personal Storyteller," *Academy of Achievement*, June 28, 1996, last updated October 22, 2006, <http://www.achievement.org/autodoc/page/tan0int-1> (January 9, 2008).

12. "Interview," *Bookreporter.com*, March 2001.

13. Amy Tan, "My Love Affair With Vladimir Nabokov," *The Opposite of Fate* (New York: G. P. Putnam and Sons, 2003), p. 221.

14. Ibid., pp. 221–222.

15. Personal interview with Amy Tan, October 31, 2006.

16. Ibid.

17. Ibid.

Glossary

cache—A hiding place.

conspire—To plot.

deport—To banish from a country.

impetus—A driving force behind an act.

leukemia—Cancer of the bone marrow.

libretto—The text or lyrics of an opera.

linguistics—The study of language.

Lyme disease—A disease caused by the bite of a deer tick that causes joint pain, fatigue, and sometimes neurological disturbances.

neuroborreliosis—A neurological disturbance characterized by memory loss and, sometimes, hallucinations.

parody—A humorous imitation.

pesticides—Chemicals used to destroy plant fungi or pests.

posttraumatic stress—Continued anxiety and fear experienced after a traumatic event.

remainder—A book discounted by its publisher when sales are minimal.

solace—Comfort.

Further Reading

Darraj, Susan Muaddi. *Amy Tan*. New York: Chelsea House, 2007.

Loos, Pamela. *A Reader's Guide to Amy Tan's* The Joy Luck Club. Berkeley Heights, N.J.: Enslow Publishers, Inc., 2008.

Martin, Michael. *Chinese Americans*. New York: Chelsea House, 2003.

Rosinsky, Natalie M. *Amy Tan*. Minneapolis, Minn.: Compass Point Books, 2007.

Internet Addresses

Amy Tan's Official Web site
  http://www.amytan.net/

**Redroom.com, Amy Tan maintains a Web page
  at this Web site.**
  http://www.redroom.com/author/amy-tan

Amy Tan biography from her literary agency
  http://www.barclayagency.com/tan.html

Academy of Achievement Amy Tan biography
  http://www.achievement.org/autodoc/page/tan
  Obio-1

Index